Kargil
35°

Dras
35°

PUBLIC
NATIONAL
VALID IN
J.K. PUNJAB HARYANA
BIHAR, W. BENGAL.
JKE 517   GUJRAT.
           ANDRA.

CARRIER
PERMIT
THE STATE
CHD. DELHI, U.P. M.P.
ASSAM, RAJASTHAN
MAHARASHTRA,
KARNATKA,

Sonamarg
34°

Leh
34°

INDIAN STYLE

JKE 517

SUPER
FAST

JKE
517

Thikse

34°

Delhi

29°

Chandigarh

31°

Simla

31°

INDIAN STYLE

By Suzanne Slesin and Stafford Cliff

Photographs by David Brittain
Foreword by Ismail Merchant and James Ivory
Introduction by Steven R. Weisman

Design by Stafford Cliff
Art Associate: Ian Hammond
Research Associates: Ann Mytton and Michael Henry Adams

Thames and Hudson

TO MICHAEL STEINBERG
JONATHAN SCOTT
JAN BRITTAIN

First published in Great Britain in 1990 by Thames and Hudson Ltd, London

Originally published by Clarkson N. Potter, Inc., 201 East 50th Street, New York, New York 10022

Printed and bound in Japan

ACKNOWLEDGMENTS

First of all we would like to thank Maggie Heaney, who suggested the idea of *Indian Style;* and second, Priscilla Carluccio, for all her help and guidance, and the dozens of names and introductions she provided.

We also thank Michael Adams and Ann Mytton, for their research; Pallavi Shah, of Air India in New York, who graciously offered invaluable expertise and comments; Steven R. Weisman, who provided his acute observations India as a longtime correspondent in that country for the *New York Times;* and Ismail Merchant and James Ivory, wh as international filmmakers and longtime observers contributed their unique points of view in the Foreword. Many others deserve our gratitude for their help in the preparation of *Indian Style*: Jacqueline Ayer; Katherine Bar at Explorasia; B. B. Bhasin; Ellen Chesler; Elizabeth Drake a Spencer Scott Travel; Leyland Gomez, Michael Green, and Ferouk Kapadia at Air India; Derek Malcolm, Mr. G. Ramamurthi, and Mrs. Manjeet Dhillon at the Governmen of India Tourist Office in London; and Jo Ann Secor.

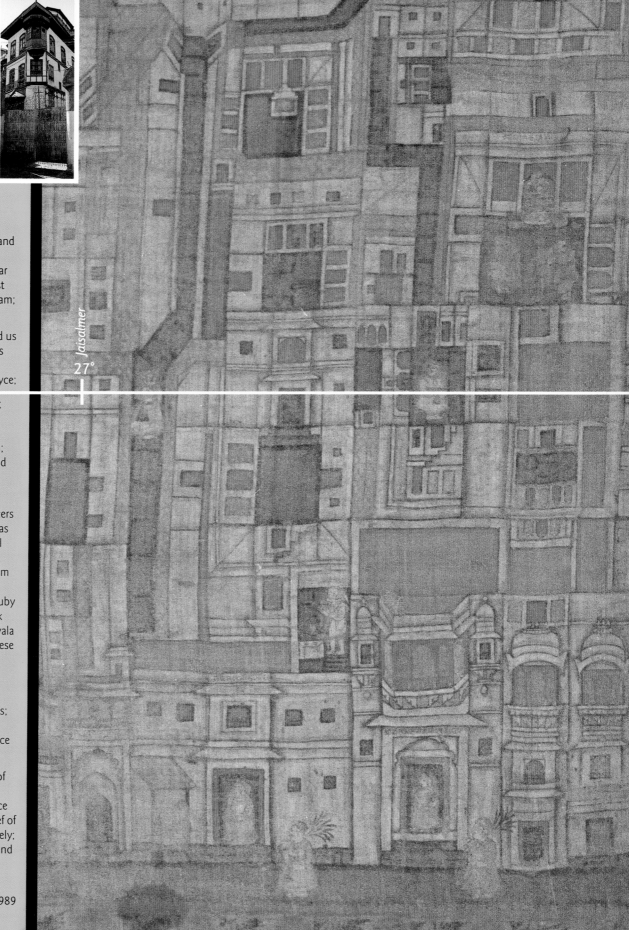

In India, we are indebted to those who helped with ideas and suggestions, who introduced us to friends and took us to houses. They include Mohammed Ashraf; Sheila Balaji; Mohammed Bass; Elizabeth Beck; John Bissel at Fabindia; the Calico Museum of Textiles; Khotty Chenai; Matin Chunka; B. V. Doshi; Rashid Gosani of the Johansen Travel Agency in Srinagar; Alok Jain at the Umaid Bhawan Palace in Jodphur; Pupul Jayakar, Nayana Kathpalia, and Hershad Kumari at the Indian National Trust; Sammy Malik, Mani Mann, Naomi Meadows, and Mario and Habiba de Miranda; Aman Nath; Marianne Pereira at the Hyatt Regency Hotel in Delhi; Dominique Radakrishnan; Asha and Suhrid Sarabhi; Mallika Sarabhai and Biphin Shah at Mapin Publishing; Mohy Yaqub Babgazim Shah; Arvind Sharma at the Hotel Shiv Shekhawati; Kanwar Ratanjit Singh; Mortand Singh at the Indian National Trust for Art and Cultural Heritage; Th. Sunder Singh; Bijoy Sivram; Ahmed Wangoo; and Francis Wacziarg.

To those who welcomed us into their homes and allowed us to take photographs, and particularly, those whose homes because of restricted space had to be left out of the final selection: Raja Atal; Christian Fellens; Dhanalakshmi Fordyce; Prameshivar and Adi Godrej; Shanta Guhan; Satish Gujral; Sudhri Kilachand; A. T. Kunjachan; Smt. Lilavati Lalbhai; Harsh Vadam Mangaldas; Ritem Muzumdar; Aster Patel; N. C. Roy; Ram Sharma; Gerbachan Singh; Patwand Singh; Thakur Bikram Singh; Anuradha Vasudev; and Wilfried and Mrinalina Vogeler.

We are also grateful for the support and guidance of the Department of Tourism and its various divisions and officers all over India, both in helping to arrange our trips as well as providing accommodation and guides. Particularly helpful were Mr. Bhaskar in Bangalore; A. B. Deenadayalu in Pondicherry; Mrs. Devichand at the Department of Tourism in Bombay; Mr. S. K. Misra, Mr. Goswami, Mrs. Nair, and Mr. K. C. Dogra at the Department of Tourism in Delhi; Ruby Palchoudhuri at the Crafts Council of West Bengal; Arunk Sood at Himachal Tourism; Kirti Thakar and N. C. Matarwala and the Tourism Corporation of Gujarat; and Babu Varghese at the Trivandrum Department of Tourism.

In London, we owe thanks to Bill Johnstone and Laurie Weavers at Trucolor; Stephen Dalton, photographic assistant to David Brittain; Dave Halliday at Leeds Cameras; Ian Hammond, Production Coordinator; Andrew Petit at Brandprint; Tony Tortoroli at Campaign Color; and Maurice White at Front Page Graphics.

And in New York, we appreciate the continuing support of Lucy Kroll, our agent; Barbara Hogenson and Karen Kligerman at the Lucy Kroll Agency; Alan Mirken and Bruce Harris of Crown Publishers; Carol Southern, editor-in-chief of Clarkson N. Potter; and especially our editor, Lauren Shakely; Pamela Reycraft; and all the others at Clarkson N. Potter and Crown who participated in the creation of this book.

Suzanne Slesin, New York
Stafford Cliff, London   November 1989

Jaisalmer
27°

CONTENTS

FOREWORD

By Ismail Merchant
and James Ivory

When I was growing up in Bombay, no one ever talked about style as it applies to people's houses. There were large houses, where industrialists and movie stars and people like that lived, and there were the other kind, graduating downward in size, where everyone else lived, including myself. All of these habitations, great or small, were at the mercy of Bombay's habitual heat. Every house had blackened peeling walls, including those of millionaires. You didn't notice that because every house mildewed in the monsoon. When you took fresh-starched clothes out of the almirah, they were already damp and drooping, and the pages of the books got spots on them that never came out. Periodically, men came to whitewash the blackening walls, most often washing them with a bright blue distemper. My father always had our walls brightened with oil paint because it lasted longer.

When I was about two, my parents, who had been living with my grandmother, moved into a small apartment in the middle of the Bhindi Bazaar, an area inhabited by many *Memon* Muslims, the community to which I belong. The apartment house was five stories tall, with two apartments to a floor. Our family consisted then of my parents, my three elder sisters, and myself. In time, three more daughters arrived. Until my older sisters were married, nine of us lived in two rooms, not counting the kitchen and bath. One of these two was my parents' bedroom, but sometimes it overflowed when relatives came to visit. For furniture there was a double bed and a big clothes cupboard, called an almirah (a Portuguese word), and some small trunks along the walls and under the bed. The other room – the living room (in Bombay this room is called the "hall") – was where my sisters and I usually slept, on seven thin matresses laid out on the floor. During the day these were rolled up and stored away. There was a sofa covered in leather, a sort of club sofa. To say it was Art Deco would be too grand. What seemed grand, to our eyes, was my mother's glass-fronted cabinet of small treasures. There were odds and ends of silver in it, pieces of china and glass, dolls, souvenirs – the kind of collections seen everywhere in the world in middle-class people's houses.

My father sometimes liked to sleep out on the balcony, and at night the servant lay down on the kitchen floor. In those days there was no refrigerator and no modern stove, or other appliances apart from the sink. The cook worked over a spirit stove, or even a bucket of coals. Since nothing could be refrigerated, only what could be consumed in a day was brought home from the markets and cooked. Ice came up from the bazaar when we needed it to make cold drinks. Sometimes the cooking was done outside on the stair landing. When we ate, a mat was laid out on the kitchen floor spread with the dishes and we all sat on it in a semicircle. We did not go in much for pictures and things like that. There was a framed view of the *durgah* at Amjer, the shrine to Khawja Mohinuddin Chistie, the favored saint of our family. There was also, of course, a picture of the Kaaba at Mecca. When I think of how today my own walls are jammed with all sorts of pictures I hardly bother to glance at, and my rooms filled with useless furniture, I wonder how this could have happened. When I see Bombay apartments now and compare them with the one I grew up in – I'm speaking of quite modest ones, nothing fancy – I am struck by the buying mania of middle-class Indians, with their passion for color television, kitchen gadgets, and glitzy-looking telephones, not to mention big refrigerators, which have been replaced in the hall by the VCR as today's status symbol. All we had was a radio made in India by a company called Chicago Radio. Our rooms were full of people, rather than things.

Beyond our cramped apartment – really an extension of it – was the biggest room of all, the street, where so many Indians do so much of their living. Millions of my countrymen seem unconcerned to carry on the sort of domestic routine that usually goes on inside. The commonest of these, which every tourist notices, is outdoor bathing: people washing themselves from a spigot in a courtyard or a broken water main in a street, or perhaps ritually on the banks of the rivers Jumna and Ganges. Another common sight is of people fast asleep out in the open, usually on rooftops, sometimes on the lawn, and (too often) in the street, when there is no other place to lie. For people with a rooftop, *charpoys*, basic Indian beds, are brought out on summer nights before the monsoon arrives, and the whole family lies together under the stars. When Indians go abroad, this is one of the things we miss the most. Or perhaps it is the memory of past family closeness in the proximity of those many beds.

My sister Amina had some rather grand in-laws. She married into the family of Sir Suleman Kasam Mitha, who had been knighted by the British for the conciliatory role he played among Indian Muslims at the turbulent time of Indian Independence. The Mitha family occupied a very large bungalow in the Nepean Sea neighborhood, next to the Aga Khan's. It has since been pulled down and replaced by a high-rise luxury apartment house. I think this was the first big house I was ever taken to. This vanished bungalow was approached by a flight of marble steps which led up to a wide veranda also paved in marble. There was a lot of comfortable rattan furniture, and I

 x

Manhattan 16°

Madras 13°

remember the cool breezes that never stopped blowing through that veranda no matter what the season. It extended very near to the sea, and during the monsoon the booming of the angry waves could be heard clear and loud on the veranda of Amina's in-laws, and sometimes the spray even dampened our faces.

When I was older – a college student – I went to a house forever associated in my mind with glamour, that of the movie actress Nimmi, who was then, in the mid-1950s, at the height of her fame. Her living room was custom-fitted with shiny built-in sofas covered in red velvet, and on these there were red velvet cushions piled up. In front of the sofas there were big glass-topped coffee tables, and to complete her ensemble, or complement it, was a crystal chandelier. Everything seemed to be all glass and shiny wood, and the whole place shone as a movie star's house should.

Since those days I think I've been in every style of Indian house, in every part of the land, visiting them either as a filmmaker in hopes of finding an interesting set, or because, as a filmmaker, people want to meet me. Even the social invitation becomes a sort of informal location prowl, and I have spent much of my time in other people's homes simply looking at how they live and arrange their rooms, storing this for future use.

Ismail Merchant

My first impressions of Indian style – that is to say, of the kind of Indian houses and interiors shown in this book – could only come by way of seeing films. Before I had become interested in things Indian, I saw Jean Renoir's *The River* when I was a student in my early twenties living in Los Angeles. There for the first time I saw the colonial planter's bungalow (unless you want to count the Hollywood one in the Bette Davis movie *The Letter*), with its verandas hung with *cheeks* – long bamboo blinds – and its darkened rooms full of old rosewood furniture through which bare-footed family servants moved softly. I don't know how authentic it was, whether these sets were shot in India or in some studio far away in the West, without benefit of local expertise or local props. I know the fine Indian art director, the late Bansi Chandragupta, worked as a very young man on that film in some capacity in its art department.

Chandragupta was totally responsible, however, for the sets in Satyajit Ray's *Pather Panchali,* which I saw a few years later. The locale was the same – Bengal – but the setting had moved away from the lordly lifestyle of an English planter of hemp to that of an appallingly poor Brahmin family living in a broken-down house in a rural village. The floors were mud, I think, the roof was thatched, doors hung off their hinges, and tattered blinds could

not keep out the storm. Light coming from an oil lamp provided the means for the ancient auntie to throw magical shadows on the wall.

These two films shared more than Bansi Chandragupta: both were highly lyrical works by two of the very greatest film directors who ever lived, one well toward the end of his career, the other at the very beginning. To this day I often judge a certain kind of Indian room – it does not have to be in a film – not by what it is, but by what Satyajit Ray has shown, first in his "Apu" films, and then in others like *The Music Room, Charulata,* and *The Chess Players.*

Then I began looking at another kind of Indian room: those depicted in Indian miniature paintings, rooms associated with royalty. But not a savage sort of royalty, such as we find in sinister 19th-century photographs of crazed maharajas, but of an earlier and a purer, nobler sort, a realm from which diminutive kings and queens seemed to be showering down graces on their subjects. Their personages – sometimes they were divinities, or surrogates for divinities – inhabited spare, white, almost empty rooms, where the only furniture might be *charpoys* – the basic Indian bed – with legs of gold or ivory. There was always a thick bolster on this bed. A scarlet or yellow curtain was often furled, ready to drop when the royal couple lay down. Behind and above this couch were niches in which there stood a perfect flask and two little wine cups, or blue and white vases, or a bouquet of flowers. Sometimes the walls were decorated with chaste patterns - arabesques and floral designs, which were austere and playful at the same time. None of these pretty rooms ever had anything more than a bed in it - no traditional Indian palace room ever did, unless it was a *takht,* also a kind of bed you might say, actually a sort of platform comfortably padded and covered with white sheets, on which any number of people could loll against bolsters and converse or take tea. In these rooms there might be a box, or a mirror, sometimes a very low table, for Indian kings and queens, when not lounging on a *takht,* sat on the floor like their subjects, on a carpet laid over a striped dhurrie.

The traditional Indian interior has always been floor-oriented as in Japan. The reader may forget this about India. It isn't a place like China, with a variety of fine, sophisticated pieces of furniture such as we have in the West. Western furniture is an acquired taste in India, an importation by the various European colonists - English, Portuguese, Dutch, and French. By the 19th century, when rich Indians wanted to entertain these overlords, or to emulate or outdo them, they ordered suites of furniture. But there is scarcely an Indian today, no matter how Western-educated or widely

traveled, who is not perfectly comfortable sitting crosslegged on a floor, or even sleeping on it in a pinch, and rising the next morning with no apparent ill effects.

The next Indian rooms I knew about were actually in India: or rather, I was in them, at last, in India. The first of these I encountered tended to be the modern, rather too refined houses and apartments of very Westernized Indians in New Delhi and Calcutta, though in the latter city these habitations were less self-conscious and more serious. They contained modern wicker furniture and folk paintings and chunks from the temples at Khajuraho, mixed in with small smart-looking inexpensive objects from stores in New York, or found in London's Portobello Road. But for all their seeming a little precious to me on later reflection, at the time these places seemed abodes of peace and tranquillity after my long trip to the Rajasthan desert.

Ismail has just written about the outdoor room, the room without walls. A version of this - more often, though not exclusively, to be found adjoining the homes of the better-off - is what might be called the garden room. Indian miniature paintings often show these: a small formal garden with a fountain or a little trickling waterway, natural or man-made. You can of course sit there in the shade doing nothing more than appreciating the sound

of moving water on a hot day, but you can also do accounts, type a letter, meet business people, arrange a marriage, or - as the history books tell us - order the execution of an enemy or plan a battle. If you want to wash your hands before eating there, you may summon a servant who pours water over them from a ewer into a basin. So refined is this kind of Indian ablution, you do not even have to see the sullied water as it falls from your hands: fresh green leaves are arranged over a kind of flat, upside-down colander in the basin, through which the soapy water drains. The servant then gives you a little hand towel. A variant of the garden room is the modern Indian reception alfresco - a dim memory, like the hand washing, of nomadic times and tent living - in which guests are entertained on sofas and chairs dragged out on the lawn and arranged formally on carpets, along with small tables and even floor lamps, all brought from inside the house. This, too, is very much in the Indian style.

In my first travels around India, I went into a special, a very particular, kind of house: that of the art dealer. Whether in a big city like Calcutta, or a small one like Jaipur, the style there - and the courtesies - were the same. You sat - sometimes on a hard sofa or chair, sometimes on the floor on a white sheet - drinking Coke or tea, while piles of old miniature paintings were put in front of you.

These were kept in a tin trunk, or in a suitcase, or in the almirah, and were produced tied up in red cloth bundles. The pictures were often in terrible condition, from attack by white ants and moisture, and all but fell to pieces in your hands. It would get dark outside and the lights - or light - would be turned on: one bulb high up on a luridly painted wall. From somewhere inside the house or apartment would come mysterious sounds. You never met the art dealer's ladies. There would be shouts and bangings from the street, and several different film songs jumbled up, coming from other houses or perhaps a passing wedding procession. The art dealer chewed paan and spat into a little spitoon as you considered. Sometimes a bird flew in and spattered a picture you were holding. If you didn't have enough money you took your purchase away with you and later the dealer's man came to see you at your hotel, however far that might be. In those far-off days, everybody trusted you.

James Ivory

As partners in Merchant Ivory Productions, Ismail Merchant and James Ivory have made many of their films in India, together with the writer Ruth Jhabvala, including the classic *Shakespeare Wallah.* Most of these films, like that one, were set in the present day and had to do with the social phenomenon that is the Englishman Abroad. But sometimes it is the Englishwoman Abroad, as in the more recent *Heat and Dust* - the theme explored from another angle, and in another country, in *A Room with a View.*

Mysore 12°

INTRODUCTION

By Steven R. Weisman

If there is such a thing as an epiphany that can crystallize the experience of living in India, mine was at the fabulous Hindu religious festival at Hardwar on the banks of the Ganges River in the Himalayan foothills. On a sultry day at dawn, the air was heavy with the pungent fragrance of cardamom, lotus blossoms, and hashish as hundreds of holy men, with long matted hair and flowing beards, many of them naked, marched into the river for their ritual baths.

These holy men, or sadhus, had come from their ashrams in the dense forests or mountain caves where they live in silence. In the evening, other Hindu pilgrims lit tiny candles, set them on leaf boats, then pushed them off across the surface of the water, so that the scattered, bobbing flames mirrored the canopy of stars overhead.

The Hardwar festival, embodying the odd mixture of tawdriness and spirituality that is India, commemorates a legendary battle between gods and demons over a vessel of sacred nectar, which, according to the Hindu scriptures, spilled at twelve spots in the universe, four on earth and eight in the heavens. I have always thought ever since that the ratio was about right: at least two-thirds of India must be taken on faith.

Perhaps this is why writers caught up in India struggle so hard to describe being overwhelmed by vast spaces and multitudes of humanity, and even more by the immense world of the Indian spirit. Of course, Indians work every day in the real world to lift themselves out of the wretchedness and suffering that has been their lot for centuries. But Indian philosophy is also rooted in deeper principles of immersion, abandonment of the self, and finally, acceptance. Before thinking about India, Westerners have to clear their minds of prejudice, unclench their fists, and look beyond the miseries and splendors of the surface.

In a famous formulation cited by Sigmund Freud, the novelist Romain Rolland spoke of the "oceanic feeling" of India. That same essence was captured even more perceptively by the psychoanalyst Erik H. Erikson, who in his biography of Mohandas K. Gandhi suggested that India exists in a kind of feminine space, as if Father Time in India were a woman. Erikson spoke in this context of the "sense of being enveloped, embedded, and carried by the world."

India is a country of 800 million people, thousands of gods, hundreds of castes, dozens of languages and dialects, and several

LEFT: A shopper buys her fresh vegetables from one of the dozens of men and women who gather each day with their homegrown produce at Sardar market in the old city in Jodhpur, Rajasthan.

of the world's great religions. It traces its history back to settlements on the Indus River nearly 5,000 years ago, has been conquered, invaded, or subjugated since the days of Alexander the Great, and became a modern nation-state in 1947, when the British partitioned the former empire on the Asian subcontinent into the new countries of India and Pakistan. This much is fundamental. But I often told American friends that one must start in India by accepting the difficulty of ascertaining "facts."

Among India's masses, for example, grinding poverty and pervasive spirituality have long since warped what we in the West think of as distinctions between what is real and what is not. No less an authority than Jawaharlal Nehru, the nation's founding prime minister, observed in his own history of India, written while he was serving a prison term during the struggle for independence, that ancient Indians – unlike ancient Greeks, Chinese, or Arabs – did not write what Westerners would regard as factual accounts of kings, wars, and conquerors. Instead they left only narratives of fantastic gods and heroes and demons. It would be as if the only history bequeathed to us from ancient Greece were contained in Greek mythology. "This imagined history and mixture of fact and legend became widely known and gave to the people a strong and abiding

cultural background," Nehru wrote. "But the ignoring of history produced a vagueness of outlook, a divorce from life as it is, a credulity, a wooliness of the mind where fact was concerned."

Fantastic legends and histories are today spread across the sacred landscape traversed by religious pilgrims following in the footsteps of saints and holy men of thousands of years ago. I was entranced by the seductive power of Indian holy places. At the riverbank at the northern India town of Mathura, Krishna, the most popular god in the Hindu pantheon, stole the clothes of a group of milkmaids bathing nude in the river, then seduced them by playing his flute and dancing in a shadowy glade. I have seen groups of Indian women giggling yet reverent as they ventured to bathe at the same riverbank, breathing life into this erotic legend of surrender before God. Today the story of Krishna and the milkmaids also unfolds in Indian classical dance, a revived art that brings together the sensuous and the divine.

The world of the spirit, of ghosts and demons, reaches into the mundane lives of most Indians, occasionally making communication difficult. I once asked a widow how her husband had died, only to hear her explain that he had urinated under a tree inhabited by an evil spirit. Another time, I asked a villager to give me an example of something that had

happened to him recently, either good or bad, that had been the will of God. He looked at me impatiently and explained, as if to a slow-witted child: "It's a strange question. Nothing happens on this earth unless it is the will of God." That same faith compels even the most politically sophisticated and Western-educated Indian to consult astrologers, mystics, or gurus before undertaking important decisions or ceremonies.

Indians will tell you that the vast and varied continuum of the universe manifests itself even in their style of dress. They will tell you that a man's dhoti, or flowing loincloth, and a woman's sari, tied and wrapped from a single, unstitched cloth, is continuous and flowing like the holy Ganges River. Indian dress may be unique to India, but the eclectic architecture of India draws from a hundred different traditions and influences. There are the astonishing palaces and tombs, such as the Taj Mahal, left by the Moguls; churches in the south bearing the influence of Spain and Portugal; forts and ramparts of Rajasthan inspired by the splendor of ancient Persia; soaring towers of Hindu temples like the one at Madurai covered with intricate, labyrinthine sculptures evoking myths and legends; or the huge overhanging roofs and open spaces of a teak maharaja's palace in south India whose Chinese influence speaks of trading activity

centuries ago. Yet the most typical Indian architectural style is extremely practical. An Indian official once explained to me that Western consultants had proposed razing mud huts in the Himalayan foothills and replacing them with sheds of solid concrete. But the villagers found that they could not live in the fancy new concrete sheds because they failed to insulate them from the cold the way the old mud huts did. Equally practical, of course, are the thatched roofs of banana and coconut leaves in the south, or the slum dwellers' huts made of old drainage pipes or discarded shipping crates.

The Indian's own response to the profusion of life seems to take two routes. First is the endless cataloguing of rules and rituals, including those of bathing and preparing for prayers and religious ceremonies. A mania for organizing life can be found in the countless distinctions of language, caste, and religious sects and gods. Even the famous erotic Indian sculptures are, at one level, an almost out-of-control attempt to list and categorize every conceivable sexual position as a metaphor for the wild abundance of humanity.

Yet beneath the tumult lies the second response of seeing the basic inclusiveness and unity of life. The same Hindus who spin countless stories of gods and demigods often agree that their religion is basically monotheistic, and that all its different identities are manifestations of an unseen single divine Being whose world is more real than the transitory divisions we experience on earth. One way to reach that Being is to set aside the trappings of the world and pare human expression down to the barest essentials.

Among holy men, this impulse leads to renunciation and nakedness, the search for *om*, the beginning and end symbolized by the famous mantra of one syllable chanted still by men of God. It is no accident, the Indians say, that ancient Indian mathematicians first invented the concept of zero and made modern mathematics possible. I will also always associate that zero with the beginning of Indian ragas, which start with a smoky wisp of music as if some kind of primordial silence were slowly giving birth to sound. Indian music imparts a feeling of time itself being invented before the listener.

Time in India has its own formless qualities, perhaps because India is a country that exists in several different centuries at once, from the Stone Age to the Middle Ages to the Space Age. The elusiveness of time is not simply that in Hindi the same word is used for both "yesterday" and "tomorrow," or the fact that in some ancient Vedic texts in Sanskrit, the future is described in the past tense (analogous to "far away and a long time ago . . ." in the futuristic film *Star Wars*. No, it

is a feeling of disorientation that used to come to me when I visited the northern Indian village of Gurha. There, at the home of one of the village's dwellers, I used to bathe out of a bucket drawn from a well and sit for dinner on a mud floor "disinfected" by cow dung, enjoying mutton curry that had been cooked over a mud hearth and made savory by spices ground on a stone mortar. It was there that villagers told me about the blessings and curses of modernization, of how their children could now go to school, but graduated with new greed for possessions - a motor scooter, a digital watch, a polyester skirt. These discussions took place around a fire, since few of the mud-and-brick homes had electricity. Yet nearby, one neighbor who did have electricity was watching a televised cricket match broadcast from London.

India is thus being transformed by the rush of the modern world, but the wildly varied impact of progress is both appalling and inspiring. As the historian Romila Thapar told me: "Because so much of the past has survived, the changes India is undergoing are really so traumatic that one doesn't know which way the future is going." The challenge India faces is to modernize and cope with the effects of modernization, to ensure that development does not wreck its environment or undermine its spirit and culture, or introduce

dangerous new inequities into Indian society. Of course India may take solace in its success so far. For despite the daily infighting among its subgroups, India has maintained its national unity, forging a secular democracy and banishing the old specter of famine, though not the lingering reality of malnourishment and poverty as judged by today's Western standards.

The important lesson of India always struck me during the times that I took Western guests first into the noisy and raucous bazaars of Old Delhi, the streets teeming with hawkers, beggars, worshipers, and shopkeepers - the humanity of India, the humanity of the world. Then we would always go to the cremation site of Mahatma Gandhi, surely one of the towering figures of this century. Father of modern India, apostle of nonviolence, a prophet who urged his country and indeed the world to turn away from materialism and search for a new kind of brotherhood, Gandhi gave to the world a set of ideals that seem more urgent than ever in the nuclear age.

Gandhi's modest shrine will always be for me one of the most moving places on earth, a serene enclave where lines of humble Indians stand in silence before the simple polished granite slab and the eternal flame, touching the memorial with their fingertips, folding their hands and bowing their heads. I used to stand and

stare as they filed by. I remember a young family that turned to walk away, the father observing me observing him. He nodded and smiled so deeply that I can still feel the warmth. The drama of India is that of a country wrestling every day with the deepest and most profound tides of history and culture. But in the end, we are drawn to India because of the truth of Gandhi's idea that all humanity is one.

Steven R. Weisman, currently the Tokyo Bureau Chief for the *New York Times*, was formerly the *Times* Bureau Chief in New Delhi.

INDIA THE COUNTRY

India is about extremes. Vastness, intensity, and paradox – all are qualities that describe this ancient culture. The sharp peaks of the Himalayas, the sweltering heat of the Great Indian Plain, the delicious cool of Kashmir, arid deserts and monsoons in the tropical southwest – all these contrasts and many others are commonplace in India. Tiny villages where the slow pace of life remains the same as in centuries past are connected to teeming urban centers by dirt roads that seemingly stretch to the horizon. In this land, permeated by religion and mysticism, each spectacular dawn is like a new beginning. And each twilight offers an eagerly awaited hiatus until the new day.

LEFT: Children of a small farming community outside Leh, in Ladakh, sit for a group portrait.

ABOVE: A house made of palm leaves is nestled in a palm forest near Trivandrum.

Like India itself, the country's major cities have always been unique mixtures of old and new. Wide boulevards jammed with cars give way to narrow streets that seem unchanged from centuries past. Modern skyscrapers and decaying tenements coexist in a dynamic tension.

With a natural harbor on the west coast, Bombay, the capital of the state of Maharashtra, is for most visitors the gateway to India; on the east coast, Calcutta, a sprawling industrial center, the largest and most densely populated city in India, still contains many Victorian buildings that recall its years as the capital of British India; Delhi, the British capital after 1911, became the seat of the new republic in 1950.

RIGHT: An atmospheric early-morning view toward the center of New Delhi hints at the magical grandeur of the singular city. Planned in 1911 by Sir Edwin Lutyens, England's preeminent architect of the early 20th century, New Delhi is still admired for its tree-lined axial avenues, many spacious parks, and imposing architecture and monuments.

Rain, or the lack of it, is the catalyst of the Indian climate. In Ladakh, clouds seldom pass over the high mountain ranges, and summer days are dry, sunny, and warm, followed by clear, cold nights. Water comes from glaciers and rivers, like the nearby Khatling glacier at Uttar Pradesh, where gentle rains transform the moraines into verdant pastures covered with wildflowers.

In the Great Indian Desert, the eagerly awaited monsoons sometimes fail to appear for years in succession, causing terrible drought and hardship. In West Bengal, the July and September monsoons sweep away whole sections of roadways. Umbrellas and Western raincoats are useless in these months, and local residents have devised a kind of straw armor with woven shields in order to navigate streets and roads. In the south, humid conditions create an ideal setting for growing rice and bananas.

LEFT: Salt flats in the Ran of Kutch are flooded by rainwater after the May monsoons.

BELOW LEFT: Banana and coconut palms form a high hedge behind a field of rice in Goa.

TOP RIGHT: Stone walls delineate a series of fields of barley.

TOP FAR RIGHT: The monastery at Lamayuru in the Himalayas is ringed with fields where barley grows at 12,000 feet.

ABOVE RIGHT: By September, rice, planted by hand, has been bundled into sheaves in Kashmir.

ABOVE FAR RIGHT: Arid plains stretch for miles on the Great Indian Desert of Rajasthan.

RIGHT: Groundnuts are cultivated at Madurantakam, near Madras.

FAR RIGHT: Heavy clouds create a dramatic setting over a lake in Tamil Nadu.

ABOVE: The village of Kangar, a collection of modest, flat-roofed houses, is set above the river Indus on a tiny green plateau high up in the Himalayan mountains of Ladakh.

ABOVE: The mist rises off the water at sunrise in Goa. This southwestern area of India was first annexed by the Portuguese in the early 16th century, following Vasco da Gama's first expedition. Goa remained part of the Portuguese empire for over 450 years, becoming a colorful and flourishing colony, until it was surrendered to India in December 1961, following years of intensive negotiation.

THIS PAGE: In India, a network of roads links the different areas and cities of the vast country together - straight lines leading toward a vanishing point in the rugged mountains near Ladakh or lined with swaying palm trees in Cochin, filled with people or passing a lake in Tamil Nadu.

RIGHT: A huge load of cattle feed on its way to the drought areas of Rajasthan bulges over the side of a truck. Many of India's roads are only wide enough for a single vehicle.

All over India, people and goods seem to be in constant movement. Any form of transportation is valid and ingenuity is the order of the day. Few traffic laws are observed, cows (considered sacred by Hindus) wander untethered through the streets, passengers crowd the tops of buses and trains, and entire families balance themselves like acrobats atop motor scooters.

LEFT: A procession of oxen slowly pulls heavily loaded carts along a street in Hyderabad.

BELOW LEFT: A cow drags a large lawnmower of local design outside one of the Sir Edwin L. Lutyens parliament buildings in New Delhi.

RIGHT: Bicycles, scooters, trains, boats, camels, and oxen are some of the usual methods of transporting supplies in a country where overloading is often transformed into art.

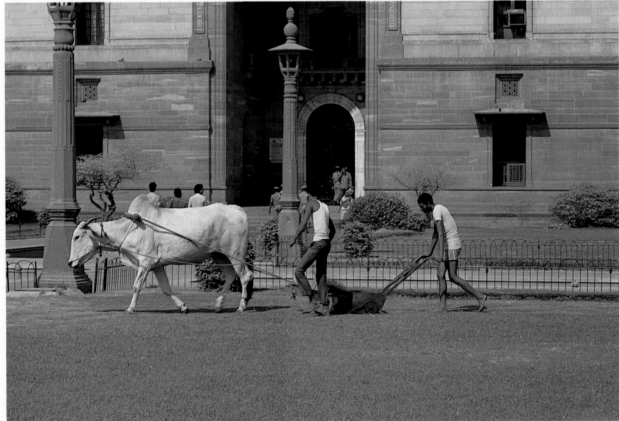

THE LOOK OF INDIA

A visit to India is most of all a startling sensual and visual experience. Everyday activities - from the enormous and seemingly chaotic yet mysteriously efficient hand laundry at the dhobi ghat in Bombay to the action-packed spectacle of street vendors offering sweets, breads, incense, even rusty nails - play a part in a panorama, apparently unchanged for centuries. One of the most magical of these daily events are the famous predawn floating markets of Kashmir. Huge pumpkins, just-picked vegetables, and brilliant flowers - poppies, cosmos, and roses - are piled high on gondolalike boats that deftly navigate the crowded lake. As in the painted

trucks that transport grain in Cochin or the diverse representations of elephants and other motifs that adorn many surfaces, the artistry of India is all-pervading.

LEFT: In Bangalore, children crowd around a street seller who threads fragrant tubor rose flowers into garlands.

ABOVE: Movie stars, depicted on giant hand-painted posters that nearly cover the walls of high-rise apartment buildings, seem to join the crowds celebrating the annual Ganesha festival in Bombay, the Indian film capital.

ABOVE AND RIGHT: In Bombay, dhobis, or washermen, cart bundles of clothing along the city streets to the dhobi ghat, the vast open-air laundry, where clothes are hand-washed. An intricate coding system, unfathomable to outsiders, allows the clothes to be returned to their proper owners.

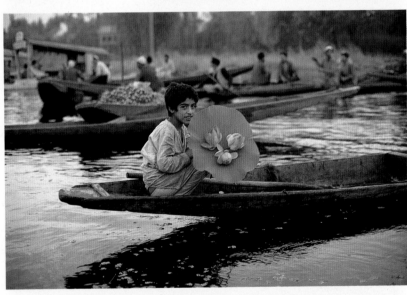

LEFT AND RIGHT: Just [before] sunrise, farmers and me[rchants in] shikaras, gondolalike b[oats,] congregate on a backw[ater of Dal] Lake in Kashmir. Veget[ables such] as turnips and carrots, [grown in] tiny kitchen gardens, as [well as] fresh flowers and huge [heads of] squash are sold to shop[keepers] amid a cacophony of bartering and negotiation. Despite their small size, most of the boats are equipped with a rudimentary scale and metal tray.

LEFT: In the villages of rural India, as well as the large modern cities, the chowk, or town square, is traditionally the center of activity - a meeting place for selling, socializing, or just passing the time. The assortment of wares at the street bazaar is limitless and can range from everyday food staples to pieces of scrap metal. There are mounds of peanuts (in Old Delhi), baskets of pomegranates, limes squeezed to order, fried bread, pastries, piles of garlic and ginger, flower garlands, children's hats, and noisemakers, and strings of plastic ducks. Even a shave - accompanied by a fastidious beard trim - is possible.

RIGHT: In Bombay's ambiance-filled Crawford market, housed in an 1871 Gothic-style building with flagstone floors and rosette-shaped windows, fruit, flowers, and vegetables are sold amid a din of shouting vendors and squawking caged birds.

TOP: In Leh, a woman sells her homegrown vegetables in the street.

ABOVE: In Trivandrum, a tiny roadside shop is bedecked with local produce - including bananas, plantains, and pineapples.

RIGHT: Door-to-door vendors, such as this one in Cochin, deliver fresh vegetables daily to the suburban houses. Okra, squash, turnips, and cabbages are some of the wares presented in a still-lifelike array that is instantly rearranged when a sale is made.

LEFT, RIGHT AND BELOW: Grain trucks, waiting to be loaded at silos in Cochin, display the brilliantly colored hand-painted decorations typical of the state of Kerala. Such slogans as "God Is Truth," "Make Love Not War," and "No Gain, No Pain" are interwoven in the fanciful interpretations of flowers and scroll-like patterns.

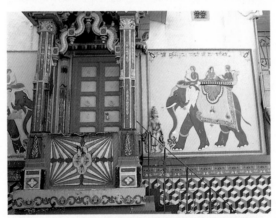

In India, the elephant has been venerated since ancient times as a sacred animal and a symbol of royalty - representing qualities of steadfastness, strength, and intelligence. Even today, the elephant - in the Hindu religion, in art and architecture, and in daily life as a benign beast of burden - is omnipresent.

Ganesha, the oldest son of Siva, and one of the most popular deities in Hinduism, has a child's body and an elephant's head. The elephant is also the subject of a myth that recounts the story of Vishnu's saving of an elephant from a demon crocodile - a parable of man's salvation from material temptation through faith.

On city streets - particularly in festivals and wedding processions, in temple compounds, and in fields and forests - the elephant acts as a powerful link between the past and the present, the spiritual and the mundane.

LEFT: Indian elephants - called kumkies *when they have been tamed - are still used for labor and, as the tallest animals, in festivals to carry the religious images. Widely represented on posters, wall paintings, and in architecture, elephants appear as stone or wood carvings on capitals, ornamental brackets, and keystones.*

RIGHT: In a house in Bissau, in Rajasthan, known as the Tibrawala haveli, an elephant's trunk forms the graceful handrail on a small staircase.

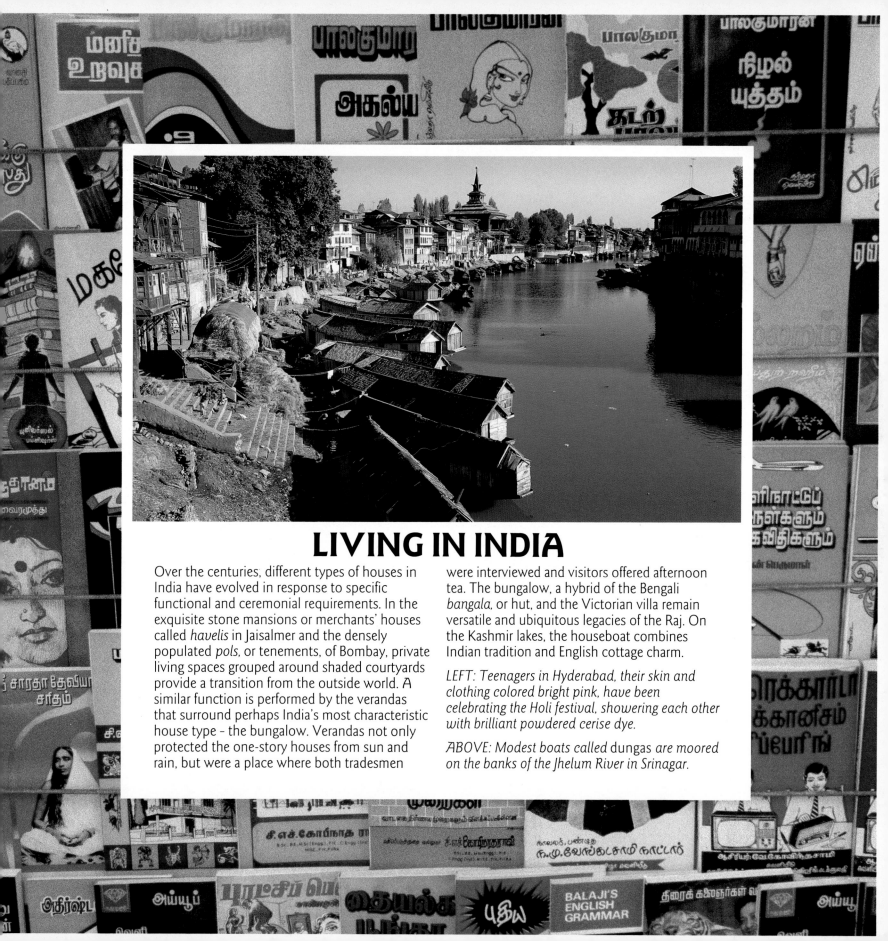

LIVING IN INDIA

Over the centuries, different types of houses in India have evolved in response to specific functional and ceremonial requirements. In the exquisite stone mansions or merchants' houses called *havelis* in Jaisalmer and the densely populated *pols*, or tenements, of Bombay, private living spaces grouped around shaded courtyards provide a transition from the outside world. A similar function is performed by the verandas that surround perhaps India's most characteristic house type – the bungalow. Verandas not only protected the one-story houses from sun and rain, but were a place where both tradesmen were interviewed and visitors offered afternoon tea. The bungalow, a hybrid of the Bengali *bangala*, or hut, and the Victorian villa remain versatile and ubiquitous legacies of the Raj. On the Kashmir lakes, the houseboat combines Indian tradition and English cottage charm.

LEFT: Teenagers in Hyderabad, their skin and clothing colored bright pink, have been celebrating the Holi festival, showering each other with brilliant powdered cerise dye.

ABOVE: Modest boats called dungas *are moored on the banks of the Jhelum River in Srinagar.*

Descendants of the rudimentary village huts of Bengal, the *bangla*, or *bangala* in Bengalese, became the English bungalow, the most ubiquitous architectural expression in India of the Raj.

Low, rambling, and usually single-story, these buildings were surrounded by open porches, or verandas, which afforded protection from the relentless sun and torrential monsoons, and took advantage of welcome breezes.

The bungalow came to be interpreted in a variety of Western styles that often reflected the tastes of the Dutch, Portuguese, and English colonial rulers. The size of the buildings was also determined by the status of their occupants. Bungalows range from the humble, with as few as two rooms under a tin roof, to the grandiose, a 40-room mansion in the Neoclassical style.

LEFT: Examples of bungalows include the Raja Atal house in Jaipur, and a garden pavilion with Neoclassical details, above far left; the Fordyce house in Bangalore, shaded by magnificent centuries-old trees, above left; Raj Bhavan, in Bombay, built between 1868 and 1877 as the official residence of the governor of Maharashtra, far left; Portuguese-influenced residences in Goa, above left, far left, and above right; and a blue-green Italianate villa in Hyderabad, left.

RIGHT: Lofty pine trees and an English-style flower-bordered walk frame a small bungalow in Simla.

Throughout the 19th century, many Indian families established great fortunes through profitable trade with the countries of Western Europe that had colonial interests in the subcontinent. In the large cities that grew from early trading posts, such as Bombay, they built stately town residences that not only were manifestations of their new stature, but also became the focus of family pride.

Reflective of a variety of European styles adapted to an Indian context, the buildings share a common enthusiasm for a lavish display of porches, porticoes, and other embellishments. Unfortunately, many are today in disrepair, while others have been either razed or converted into apartments or offices.

LEFT: Town houses, most of which were built by rich merchants, include the Lion House - so-called because of the stone carvings on the gateposts - in the Portuguese quarter of Bombay, top far left; a Gothic-style fantasy set at the end of a narrow courtyard on Malabar Hill in Bombay, top left; a Victorian Gothic town house in Hyderabad, center far left; a balconied town house in Srinagar that is reminiscent of a Swiss chalet, center left; a yellow stucco-walled residence in Bombay, far left; and an Italianate house rising above a series of arcaded shops in Mandvi, left.

RIGHT: The 200-year-old Vakil house is dramatically positioned in the heart of the old section of Srinagar, beside the Jhelum River.

ABOVE: On the top floor of the Vakil house, the enormous room once used for ceremonial occasions, such as weddings and festivals, is now empty and unused. Bay windows, with colored panes, command views over the river and the old city of Srinagar. The floor is made of a patchwork of solid-colored glazed tiles.

ABOVE: The arcaded room on the top floor
of a 100-year-old family house in Srinagar's
Rajorikadal area was once the home of Mouli
Mohamed Yousef, a famous Muslim leader.
The green banners, decorated with inscriptions
from the Koran, contrast with a geometric
pattern in the cedar ceiling.

Community living is an intrinsic aspect of Indian life. Traditionally, most Indian households – no matter their class or economic situation – included several generations of an extended family. Except for the teeming cities such as Bombay, Calcutta, and New Delhi, people of the same castes and religions have always formed separate neighborhoods.

For reasons of security as well as to satisfy such religious practices as purdah, or the seclusion of women, many buildings were planned as a series of public and private spaces. They range from the rooming house, or chawl, to the multilevel, fortresslike *haveli*. In the 19th century, imitating palaces and *havelis*, the British built large apartment blocks to house the ever-growing number of Indian civil servants. Most *havelis* and other large single-family residences have in their turn been converted into apartments. But today, all of these traditional forms of urban architecture are being replaced by high-rise apartment buildings.

ABOVE LEFT: In Jaisalmer, an elegant haveli, *with a carved stone facade, has now been divided into shops and apartments.*

LEFT: A 19th-century Bombay tenement has numerous tiny rooms, and communal washing and cooking facilities.

RIGHT: Apartment buildings in cities such as Ahmedabad, right; Jodhpur, far right; Srinagar, center right; Pondicherry, center far right; Hyderabad, below right; and Old Delhi, below far right; display architectural styles typical of their various regions - such as overhanging balconies, pointed arches, screened windows, tiled roofs, and stuccoed walls.

For centuries, the four Kashmir lakes - Dal, Nageen, Manasbal, and Wular in Srinagar - have afforded a cool respite from the long arid summers on the Indian plains. English colonists and other foreigners, prohibited by the Hindu maharajas from owning land in this resort area, spent their holidays on elaborate houseboats.

Equipped with every modern convenience, the resplendently furnished houseboats were virtually floating versions of the hill stations of Simla. Today, there are as many as 10,000 boats moored along the banks. Some, with such tempting names as *Hollywood, Buckingham Palace,* and *Queen Mum,* are available for rent by visitors as luxurious summer residences, complete with servants and cooks.

LEFT AND TOP: The Nagin Paradise with its decorative fretwork is one of the well-appointed houseboats moored on Nageen Lake in Srinagar.

ABOVE: The main saloon of the 175-foot-long and 22-foot-wide boat is lined with delicately carved paneling of scented deodar, Himalayan cedar.

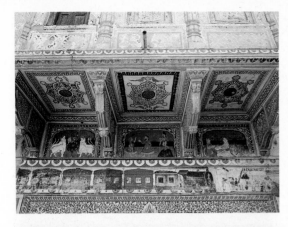

For thousands of years, the Indian culture has absorbed and adapted myriad stylistic influences. Over the course of several centuries, Islamic architecture transformed North Indian architecture. Islamic decorative traditions in carved and pierced stone - often inlaid with mirror or colored glass - and delicate miniature paintings were not only embraced by Indian craftsmen but developed into even more elaborate and detailed designs.

TOP: A 19th-century steam locomotive and train cars are depicted along with more traditional motifs under a balcony in the main room of a haveli in Jhunjhunu, Rajasthan, built by Mohanlal Ishwardas Modi about 1896.

ABOVE: In Churu, Rajasthan, painted scenes from the lives of Ganesha and Krishna top the colored-glass fanlights of the Kothari haveli.

RIGHT: A niche inlaid with antique mirror arabesques and a panel of stylized flowers is one of the brilliant focal points in the decoration of the Samode palace in Rajasthan, now converted into a hotel.

LEFT: In a bedroom in the Kothari haveli at Churu, thousands of bits of mirror are set into cornices, columns, and window surrounds to form a brilliant framework for wall paintings of Hindu deities.

LEFT: The still-bright wall paintings in the Sigtia haveli in Bissau, Rajasthan, were created in the 19th century with traditional natural pigments. Copper green, indigo, and Indian yellow were combined to depict maharajas in niches beneath a procession of horse-drawn coaches that parade around the cove of the ceiling.

RIGHT AND BELOW RIGHT: The Sigtias, who no longer live on the property, now rent rooms in the haveli to schoolteachers. With a yellow plastic electric fan and clothing strung across the muraled walls, the once sumptuous room makes an unlikely dormitory.

Color is an integral part of the visual excitement of India. Visitors often find vivid and surprising combinations of color surrounding them on buildings, in clothing – and in fact in every aspect of Indian life, disarming and sometimes even shocking. Diana Vreeland, the late American fashion authority, has called pink "the navy blue of India."

For centuries, natural colors derived from copper and even cow urine were used in painting and for textile dyes. Natural dyes are still used today to handprint cotton fabric in cities such as Ahmedabad. However, since the 1860s, when aniline dyes were first imported into India from Germany, the subtle palette of the past has extended to encompass a wide range of bold hues.

RIGHT: A carved and brilliantly colored blue-and-green stone house is set at the end of a long and narrow twisting lane in the old part of the city of Jodhpur. Shocking to Westerners, the bold and confident fluorescent hues used on many houses in the area unexpectedly enliven the dark narrow streets.

LEFT: Near the Jain temple in the walled city of Jaisalmer stands a tall and narrow ocher-colored house with a violet door and architectural details outlined in turquoise.

LEFT AND RIGHT: From Srinagar to Cochin, from Ladakh to Trivandrum, the unrestrained use of color, pattern, and texture pervades the exterior decoration of houses. The natural colors of materials such as terra-cotta tile and red Indian sandstone are juxtaposed with vibrant paints in a variety of inventive designs.

RIGHT: A small garden house, built in the 1950s near Bissau in Rajasthan, is used as a bucolic retreat by a family who have since moved into the city. Sited on a hillside, the house is surrounded by a walled garden of palm, asoka, sissoo, and neem trees. Flowers such as roses, bougainvillea, jasmine, lilies, and morning glories grow in profusion. Inside, a similar color scheme prevails in the pink-walled interior and its contrasting green-painted woodwork.

ESSENCES OF INDIA

So varied is the long history of India that no one house type can be called typical. Each is equally representative of an aspect of the country – from the traditional and ascetic Brahmin dwelling to the fortresslike merchants' houses, or *havelis*, with brilliantly colored murals depicting scenes from Hindu mythology and everyday life. Houses originally built for the British governors and civil servants also present a wide spectrum in terms of scale and style. In the hill town of Simla, grand English country houses still line the main streets of what was the summer capital of India before independence. Invariably, the style of these residences reflects a nostalgia for "home." This meant spacious living rooms filled with chintz-covered sofas, animal trophies, and potted palms. Even small houseboats – an imaginative response on the part of the British to an edict prohibiting them from owning land – present the charming paradox of the English cottage transplanted to a lake in Kashmir.

ABOVE: Electricity is the only modern touch in a palm-leaf thatched-roof house in Trivandrum.

LEFT: In the south, a group of boys crowd together, eager to be photographed.

AUSTERE COMPOUND

Part of the centuries-old Hindu religious order, the hierarchical caste system is still one of the most important aspects of Indian life. Brahmins, members of the priestly first caste, have traditionally been more powerful, wealthier, and long-lived than members of lower castes, with whom they have little contact.

Throughout India in the last few decades, Brahmin families have seen their fortunes diminished and their lands appropriated by the government. Nevertheless, many traditional Brahmin dwellings, such as the 100-year-old compound in Kerala belonging to Attupurathu Illam, still stand as a potent symbol of a proud spiritual heritage. Its simplicity and purity underscore the rigorous discipline and holy outlook of the Brahmins.

ABOVE: An elaborate mukappu, or bargeboard, enframes the gable.

TOP LEFT: The traditional house, set on a 4-foot-high concrete slab, has no exterior windows.

ABOVE CENTER LEFT: Palm branches and a large stone mortar are on the veranda.

LEFT AND RIGHT: In the central courtyard, called a talam, ceremonial objects are grouped around a hearth.

TOWN RESIDENCE

Haveli, a Persian word meaning "enclosure," was used in India to describe a spacious town residence built around an inner courtyard. The Nathamal *haveli* in Jaisalmer is particularly well known for the elaborate carvings of its balconies – the handiwork of two brothers, famous carvers of the Jaisalmer state.

Each stone slab making up the balcony is ornamented with more than two hundred different designs. Maharwal Beri Sal Singh, the ruler of the area, built the house in 1885 as a gift for his prime minister, Mohata Nathamal. Nathamal's great-grandson lives there today.

The interiors of the *haveli* combine exuberant carvings, miniature paintings in the Rajput style, and 19th-century lithographs of glamorous women.

ABOVE: The rooftop of the Nathamal haveli *commands a view of the walled city of the late 19th-century ruler Maharwal Beri Sal Singh.*

LEFT: The facade of the haveli *is composed of a series of carved* jalis, *screens of stones.*

ABOVE: The arcaded corridor has been brightly painted and gilded using stencils. The decorations frame Rajput-style portraits.

ABOVE: A 19th-century lithograph hangs above a blue-painted cabinet in the durbar hall, the main reception room.

LEFT: The balcony, with its pierced curving parapet, offered the ladies of the household a view of ceremonies held in the durbar hall. Hindu religious paintings and 19th-century European oleographs of historical subjects, as well as photographs of Indian leaders, hang above the hand-painted horizontal moldings.

ABOVE: A shuttered window in a recess in the durbar hall has a transom of blue-and-white tiles. The surrounding dazzling miniature paintings depicting court life have remained amazingly fresh in spite of the intense daylight.

Hill Station

When Rajah Charanjit Singh of Kapurthala, the present owner Ratanjit Singh's grandfather, bought Chapslee in the late 1920s, the quintessential Victorian hill station had neither indoor plumbing nor electricity. Today its facilities have been modernized, but its Old World aura remains.

Originally built in 1835 high in the hills of Simla as a summer residence for a British family, Chapslee afforded a respite from the sweltering heat of Delhi. In 1896, the property was enlarged and decorated in the high Edwardian manner with teak paneling, wood parquet floors, and a dramatic staircase.

The house was again redecorated in the late 1930s and furnished with typically modern pieces of the era.

ABOVE: Chapslee, on a crest of a hill in Simla, was built in the early 19th century.

ABOVE LEFT: In the front hall, the cut-velvet - covered sofas, Persian carpets, and floral-patterned wallpaper heighten the Edwardian setting. The portrait is of the current owner's great-grandfather.

LEFT AND RIGHT: Hunting trophies and a collection of antique arms line the red-carpeted stair and gallery. The armor came from the state armory of Kaporthala.

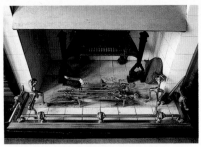

ABOVE: The drawing-room hearth depicts a romantic English landscape in glazed tile.

LEFT: Many of the furnishings and the Art Deco - patterned wallpaper in the ground-floor double drawing room date from a 1939 renovation.

LEFT: Huge carved-teak - framed mirrors, one Chinese, the other from Kashmir, flank the double doors that open onto the main entrance hall. The photographs on the tables are of contemporaries of the present owner's grandfather, including the nizam of Hyderabad and other heads of state.

ABOVE: A blackamoor cherub bracket holds an antique hammered-brass jar.

RIGHT: In the dining room, woodwork with inlaid tile and the sideboard are the only remnants of the 1896 decor. The two vases date from the 18th century.

RIGHT: A Venetian glass chandelier is suspended over the dining room table that seats 12 guests. Raja Charanjit Singh of Kaporthala was known for his elegant dinner parties and for planning the seating of his guests like a battle formation.

LEFT: Bridge was an after-dinner passion. The rug in the card room is an antique Bokhara; the legs of the small table are black buckhorns.

LEFT: The conservatory faces due west to take advantage of the afternoon sun.

RIGHT: In the Gold Room, the high Burma teak ceiling gives the sitting room the appearance of an English great hall on a small scale.

ABOVE: Faded chintz slipcovers are a nostalgic reminder of the many summers enjoyed in the house.

LEFT: The spacious bedroom suite opens onto the gallery and stair.

TOP: The magnificent brass bed in the raja's bedroom is one of the house's most notable Victorian pieces. Lace curtains frame the arch that separates the sleeping area from the sitting room.

Mountain Dwelling

Set on a plateau in Ladakh and surrounded by mountains, the house that belongs to Rigzin Padma, a schoolteacher, is one of the largest in Mulbekh.

Built twenty years ago and still incomplete, the flat-roofed, mud-covered stone house was oriented according to Buddhist traditions - facing south away from the northern winds.

In the winter, the floor below is inhabited by livestock - sheep, cows, horses, donkeys, and yaks - which help heat the living quarters.

ABOVE: Tibetan-style fretwork decorates a corner window.

TOP FAR LEFT AND TOP LEFT: Alfalfa for animal fodder is stored on the flat roofs of the houses.

CENTER FAR LEFT: Members of the Padma family stand by the entrance to the house.

CENTER LEFT: A rooftop courtyard leads to the family quarters.

FAR LEFT: Flowers grow among vegetables in the walled garden.

LEFT: In summer, all members of the household sleep on the roof.

ABOVE RIGHT: A Buddhist temple crowns the mountain.

RIGHT: The 20-year-old house reflects centuries of Tibetan architecture.

LEFT AND BELOW LEFT: An itinerant artist lived with the family for several months and painted the interior with a profusion of characteristically Buddhist motifs. These colorful decorations are a reminder of the influence of the culture of Tibet in this mountainous region of northern India. In the main room of the house, the ceiling beams and walls include dragons, peonies, and clouds.

RIGHT: The small, intricately decorated tables, called sochoks, fold flat for taking on travels. The painted wood vessels hold gram - chick-peas or dried beans.

LEFT: Guests are served tea in the still unfinished room that will eventually become a communal sleeping chamber.

BELOW CENTER LEFT: The prayer room, entered through a canopied doorway, must be higher than any other room in the house.

BOTTOM LEFT: Shoes must be removed when entering the family's elaborately painted private shrine. The altar includes a seated Buddha and four guardian deities. The ceremonial drum is struck only when a lama is present, at which time neighbors are invited to join the ritual.

RIGHT: The low ceiling of the large kitchen has blackened with the smoke from the perpetual fire in the cast-iron stove. An array of immaculately polished brass, copper, and aluminum cooking utensils is proudly displayed.

GENTLEMAN'S HOUSEBOAT

Until the end of the Raj in 1946, the houseboat moored on Nishat Lake, in Srinagar, Kashmir, was an English gentleman's summer residence. Because the British could not own land in Kashmir, these boats provided a viable housing alternative.

Made in the early 1940s and crafted of deodar wood, the boat, called the Clermont Too, is one of four owned by the Butt family. With its fretted windows and crewel-patterned linen upholstery and draperies, it might be mistaken for a cottage in the Cotswolds – were it not for the curved wooden ceilings, the sounds of lapping water, and the view of lotus leaves on the lake.

ABOVE: A gardener mows the lawn in the English-style gardens that border the lake.

ABOVE LEFT: Like neighbors on a country lane, three of the houseboats are moored beside each other on the lake.

LEFT: A double border of orange coreopsis lines the path to the front door of the houseboat.

RIGHT: The bedroom window has a view of the Himalayas and an aquatic garden of lotus leaves.

ABOVE: Bouquets of fresh flowers vie for attention with the floral Kashmiri crewel tapestrywork on the upholstery and draperies.

ABOVE: The all-white bedroom is calm and restful. The brass vessel is the only reminder of the Indian locale.

AHMEDABAD

NATIONAL SHRINE

A few miles north of the city of Ahmedabad on the west bank of the Sabarmati River stands the rustic retreat where Mahatma Gandhi, the founding father of Indian nationalism, lived with his wife, Kasturba, from 1918 to 1930.

In 1930, Gandhi left the Satyagraha Ashram with 78 of his followers to begin the famous march to the sea – a protest against the government's monopoly on salt.

Hriday Kunj, or Abode of Heart, the simple tiled-roof cottage that Gandhi built, has now been turned into a national monument. The house is preserved as it was in Gandhi's lifetime. His spinning wheel, or *charkha,* stands as a symbol of Gandhi's campaign for Indians to weave their own textiles. It still powerfully evokes the leader's opposition to English rule and economic power, and remains a poignant symbol of Indian self-determination.

ABOVE AND ABOVE LEFT: The whitewashed cottage in which Mahatma Gandhi and his wife Kasturba lived until 1930 was abandoned until local citizens decided to preserve it as a shrine.

RIGHT: In the main meeting room, Gandhi's humble sitting place, a thin white mat and simple dhadiyou, *or desk, reflect the great leader's ascetic nature.*

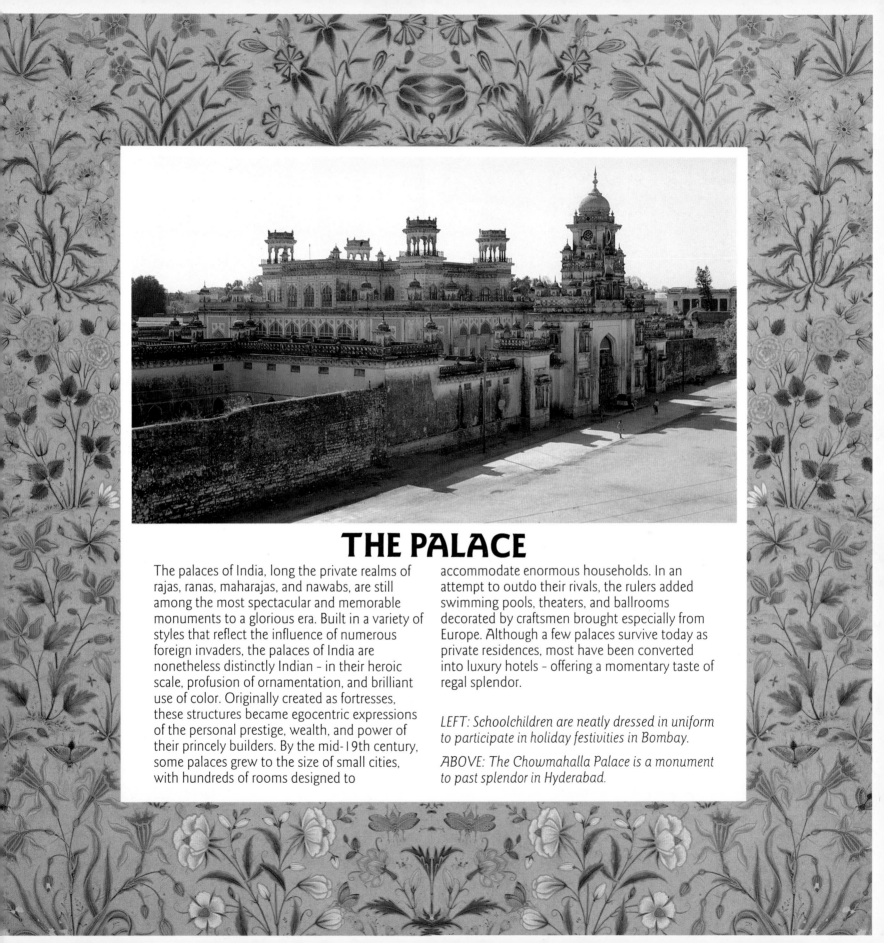

THE PALACE

The palaces of India, long the private realms of rajas, ranas, maharajas, and nawabs, are still among the most spectacular and memorable monuments to a glorious era. Built in a variety of styles that reflect the influence of numerous foreign invaders, the palaces of India are nonetheless distinctly Indian - in their heroic scale, profusion of ornamentation, and brilliant use of color. Originally created as fortresses, these structures became egocentric expressions of the personal prestige, wealth, and power of their princely builders. By the mid-19th century, some palaces grew to the size of small cities, with hundreds of rooms designed to accommodate enormous households. In an attempt to outdo their rivals, the rulers added swimming pools, theaters, and ballrooms decorated by craftsmen brought especially from Europe. Although a few palaces survive today as private residences, most have been converted into luxury hotels - offering a momentary taste of regal splendor.

LEFT: Schoolchildren are neatly dressed in uniform to participate in holiday festivities in Bombay.

ABOVE: The Chowmahalla Palace is a monument to past splendor in Hyderabad.

Anglo-Indian Splendor

Built in the 1920s near the Arabian Sea in the remote western province of Kutch, the Vijay Vilas palace is a melange of architectural styles incorporating Hindu, Islamic, and British influences.

Standing in a vast and once carefully tended formal garden, the palace seems filled with the ghosts of the past - relaxing on the pavilioned roof terraces; strolling on the shaded verandas; and peering from behind lacy marble *jali* screens.

The furnishings reflect the palace's juxtaposition of English restraint and Oriental exuberance.

ABOVE: The main driveway stretches across a flat landscape.

LEFT AND RIGHT: The 1920s Vijay Vilas palace has a bounty of architectural flourishes, including open and closed pavilions, domed towers, and ornate triple arcades.

ABOVE AND LEFT: The Italian marble floor helps keep the veranda cool and serene. The round table, surrounded by painted wicker chairs, has a top inlaid with polychrome marble depicting a wreath of flowers.

LEFT: The frosted glass-paneled doors and windows in the second-floor sitting room indicate that it was reserved for women.

ABOVE: In the Mogul tradition, the marble panels in the dining room are inlaid with colored stones in the shape of flowers.

RIGHT: The dining room, divided by a sweeping arch, can seat 20 people with ease. The chairs, with their leather seats and backs, come from Italy.

RIGHT: A hatstand made from the antlers of spotted deer and a cast-iron doorstop of an Indian soldier are on a veranda. The floor is covered in a honeycomb pattern of octagonal tiles.

LEFT: The Maharao Shri Vijay Raj Ji's bedroom on the ground floor is dominated by an Indian bed made of Burmese rosewood mounted in silver. The chaise still has its 1930s satin star-patterned fabric.

BELOW: The loggias adjoining the women's quarters are screened with a delicate fretwork of carved marble called jalis.

ABOVE: The furniture in a bedroom in the women's section was crafted in Bombay by Dewjee Canjee and Company. The bed, inspired by French Directoire, Louis XV, and English Hepplewhite furniture styles, is a good example of refined 20th-century Indian cabinet making.

LEFT AND RIGHT: On the roof, a series of enclosed and open structures offers a range of spectacular views of the domed pavilions, the gardens, and the Arabian Sea beyond.

PALATIAL RETREAT

The Narain Niwas palace on the outskirts of Jaipur was built in 1881 as a garden house or a bucolic retreat by Narain Singh-Ji, a rajput.

Designed in a fanciful version of the Anglo-Indian style popular in the Victorian Era, the palace now serves as a hotel.

One of the most appealing aspects of the decor is the typically bold color palette coupled with elements borrowed from Europe, such as crystal chandeliers and baronial four-poster beds.

ABOVE: Chairs are set out on a broad terrace.

ABOVE LEFT: The pink, yellow, and white color scheme distinguishes the main facade.

LEFT: Indian-made Morris chairs line the high-ceilinged veranda.

RIGHT: The formal arrangement of Indian Victorian and Regency upholstered furniture complements the graceful scalloped arches of the main hall.

ABOVE: Antique Afghan rugs have
been placed over the striped dhurrie
carpeting in the main hall. The
vibrant red lanterns and the opulent
chandelier were imported.

ABOVE: Ironstone china with a
chinoiserie landscape motif is
displayed in a cabinet surmounted
with an antique clock.

ABOVE: The late 19th-century
portrait over the carved sideboard
is of the Singh Kanota family, who
built the palace.

ABOVE: A display cabinet filled
with colored and cut glass forms a
transparent partition between the
dining area and the main
reception room.

LEFT: Hung with Indian brocade, the four-poster bed is part of a large suite of carved Indian-made Edwardian-style furniture.

ABOVE: In one of the imposing bedrooms, trompe l'oeil painted columns and arcades echo the architectural features of the room.

HUNTING LODGE

Maharaja Swaroop Singh and his wife Rani Usha Devi are the current occupants of Ajit Bhavan, a late 19th-century hunting palace just outside Jodhpur built for his great-grandfather, Sardar Singh.

The maharaja operates the palace as a hotel. His interest in the support and development of local artisans has led him to create a series of guest cottages in the gardens, each representing an architectural style typical of the different states of India. The palace features several grand reception rooms in which hunting trophies play a dominant role.

ABOVE: The pink sandstone facade of Ajit Bhavan forms a striking contrast with the lush greenery of the extensive surrounding gardens.

LEFT: A carved stone elephant surrounded by wicker chairs with black-and-white pillows is the focal point of the marble hall.

ABOVE: In the dining room, the Tudor-style mantelpiece, Chippendale-inspired chairs, and mounted trophies indicate the predilection for English taste.

LEFT: A vintage hand-colored photograph of hunters and their elephant tusks is framed by striking dark-blue and off-white draperies.

LEFT: The high-ceilinged living room is ringed by an assortment of furniture. A pair of elephant-foot stools and tusks flank a cocktail cabinet, converted in the 1930s from an antique family cradle. The canopy is made of thousands of strung glass beads.

ABOVE AND ABOVE RIGHT:
Silver-framed photographs of
Indian princely families are
grouped on a pair of end tables in
the living room, along with royal
presentation gifts and family
heirlooms. They include a betel
nut container in the shape of a
vintage car and a silver filigree
and jeweled elephant. The lamps
were made from Japanese vases.

FAR LEFT AND BELOW CENTER LEFT: A series of guesthouses has been built in the garden.

LEFT, BELOW LEFT, AND BELOW RIGHT: The terra-cotta and white decorative patterns on the interior of one of the guest pavilions have been based on houses in Magh. A woven-string fabric covers the doors, wardrobes, and headboards.

BELOW FAR LEFT: The random stone arcade of one of the guesthouses encloses a terra-cotta wall decoration.

BELOW LEFT: One of the bathrooms has been designed to look as if it were part of an ancient grotto.

ABOVE RIGHT: A tree trunk grows through the roof of one of the guest bedrooms. The circular room - with its beds made of old farm carts and multicolored tapestry - was inspired by houses in Shravaha.

HISTORIC FORTRESS

Cannon still guard the ramparts of Mandawa Castle, a fortress palace in the Shekhavati area of Rajasthan that has been in the same family since Thakur Nawal Singh built it in 1775. The castle has spectacular views of Mandawa's historic temples and monuments.

With its labyrinth of rooms, courtyards, and passageways built in different periods and styles, Mandawa Castle, now owned by the two brothers Randhir and Kesari Singh, is one of India's most romantic palaces. Converted into a hotel, the castle offers a rare opportunity to experience the charm of a past era.

ABOVE: The weathervane in the shape of a peacock sits atop one of the corrugated metal roofs.

TOP LEFT: Mandawa Castle offers a fairytale view of the town below.

ABOVE LEFT: On the roof terrace, coffee is served in front of a carved marble sofa.

LEFT: A member of the hotel staff sports a distinctive saffron turban.

RIGHT: Slatted blinds shade the veranda/lounge from the afternoon sun. Rattan chairs and settees and a cannon from the mid-19th century furnish the two-story outdoor room.

LEFT: Brightly colored chevron-patterned hangings and traditional bolstered seating create a romantic environment in a lounge that was once part of the palace's zenana, or women's quarters.

RIGHT AND BELOW RIGHT: The dining room has been painted an intense green with multicolored borders and decorated with braided camel bells. The arched windows are topped with stained-glass lunettes and the ceiling is hung with typical hanging lamps, called handis, which were brought to India from Europe.

LEFT: Architectural details, color, and texture contribute to the special quality of Mandawa Castle. Painted Anglo-Indian chairs, a pale yellow and white courtyard with lacy jalis, mysterious stairways, and massive brass-studded doors offer glimpses into the palace's past.

ABOVE: In one of the castle's 35 bedrooms, polished stone columns frame the Victorian iron-and-brass bed. The ceiling fan is flanked by glass lanterns.

BEAUX-ARTS PALACE

Chettinad House in Madras typifies the kind of palace built in a Beaux-Arts Neoclassical style in the early 20th century.

Designed by a German architect and completed in 1929, the 50-room compound is now the principal residence of Dr. Raja Ramaswamy, a businessman.

The spacious interiors (the dining room, for example, seats 30 people), furnished with Art Deco pieces from the 1930s as well as horse-racing trophies, impart a sense of the glamour of the last years of the Raj.

ABOVE: A festooned cartouche over the main entrance is painted with a family emblem and motto, a landscape, and a sitar.

ABOVE LEFT, FAR LEFT, AND LEFT: Chettinad House, a complex of heavily decorated buildings, wraps around a formal forecourt.

RIGHT: The palace has a panoramic view over the Ayadar River outside Madras.

112

LEFT: An imposing entry opens onto a ceremonial staircase that leads to the second floor, where elephant tusks stand at attention on the landing.

BELOW LEFT: Silver trays and cups fill the glass cases in the trophy room. The photographs also commemorate victorious polo matches and horse races.

RIGHT: The semicircular salon is furnished with damask-covered chairs and sofas.

ABOVE: A family photograph is enshrined on a table in the center of the living room.

RIGHT: In the living room, the white plaster walls contrast with the teak window frames and ceiling. The two-tone marble floor has been laid in a pattern that echoes the design of the deep-coffered ceiling.

THE FAMILY HOUSE

Devotion to family remains an enduring value in Indian society, regardless of different cultural and religious backgrounds. The family house, occupied by successive generations, reflects the family's ancestry – whether Dravidian, Jewish, Hindu, Muslim, or Catholic. In Goa, the tiled-roof stucco houses with Baroque details and private chapels reflect more than 200 years of Portuguese rule. Many houses in the Jewish area of Cochin have elements such as Delft tiles and paneled shutters introduced to the region by Dutch traders in the 17th century. Victorian villas with Gothic fretwork and arched windows, like the one built by Dr. Hasahuddim Ahmed's grandfather in suburban Hyderabad, were built by both the wealthy English and Indians during the Raj. Traditionally such residences were occupied by large households of extended family members and were passed on from one generation to the next. But more and more, the ancestral family home is becoming part of a disappearing way of life in modern India.

LEFT: In Bombay, people have crowded together to watch the Ganesha festival processions.

ABOVE: An English-style garden frames a half-timbered family house in Srinagar that has been roofed in corrugated tin.

MARGAO

HOUSE OF SEVEN GABLES

Enrico das Dores Santana da Silva was born in the 300-year-old Portuguese Rococo house known as Seven Shoulders because of its original seven gables, only three of which remain. The judge is a member of the eighth generation of a leading family of the imperial Portuguese colony in Goa: Sebastiano da Silva, who built the imposing residence in Margao, was an emissary to the Portuguese viceroy.

With its triple, tiled roof, scroll-decorated windows, wrought-iron balconies, and landscaped terrace, the house is an exceptional example of the colonial Portuguese style.

Local craftsmen using native materials adapted the interiors from Baroque designs. The pedimented double-height hall and the adjacent chapel altar and fittings came from Portugal in the 18th century, and particularly reflect the flamboyant style.

ABOVE: A dusty road with tropical plants passes the house in Margao.

ABOVE LEFT: The two-toned facade, divided into nine bays, is set behind a series of terraces.

LEFT: The windows that overlook the front garden have slatted shutters of translucent oyster shells.

RIGHT: The private chapel, one of the first in Goa to be consecrated, is dedicated to Saint Anne. It is set in an arched recess on the half landing. Terra-cotta and polychromed portrait reliefs fill the pediments in the hall.

RIGHT: A zigzag-patterned floor, stenciling, and blue-and-white Chinese Export ware create an informal setting in the entrance. The unusual-looking antique seat is a double rocking chair.

ABOVE: European and Chinese ceramics from the 18th and 19th centuries have been arranged on a marble-topped console table in the drawing room. Carved and gilded wood hands once held large mirrors shipped from Europe.

RIGHT: The drawing room was once part of an enormous salon with room for 200 guests. With its austere white walls, black-and-white terrazzo marble floor, and ebonized rosewood furniture, it is both stylish and refined. Gold and scarlet brocaded damask fabric hangs from early-19th-century arrow-shaped rods.

ABOVE: Decorative plasterwork frames the doorways in the tiled-floor bedroom. The painted iron-and-brass Victorian bed has a half tester draped with lace.

*ABOVE: Blue-and-white Chinese
Export porcelain stands out in
relief against a red background in
a small sitting room.*

ABOVE: The glittering array of heirloom silver is kept in a glass-fronted cabinet in the dining room.

RIGHT: Hanging lamps (handis) and a cut-glass chandelier hang from the center of the latticed ceiling of the green dining room.

TROPHY ROOMS

In Jodhpur, the 144-year-old Pal House, owned by Bhawani Singh of Pal, is an evocative example of the *haveli*, an impressive merchant's mansion built around a central courtyard.

All-male parties, with the women of the house in jourdah, and formal celebrations were once held in the second-floor reception room. Trophies and photographs covering the walls recall the family's active past.

ABOVE: Edwin Lord Weeks painted the 19th-century haveli in 1887, when the mansion was a center of trading activity.

LEFT: One of the current occupants of the house stands on the stairs that link the courtyard to the rooms above.

ABOVE RIGHT: The two-tone facade of the house rises dramatically above the small shops and main bazaar in the center of the town.

ABOVE FAR RIGHT: A majestic old tree shades the courtyard.

RIGHT: Younger members of the family and their friends pose in front of earlier family photographs.

RIGHT: Hunting trophies and photographs of shooting parties decorate the painted and gracefully arcaded hallway.

BELOW RIGHT: Mirrored glass balls hang from the beamed wooden ceiling in the grand reception room.

LEFT: An old rifle barrel has been transformed into a standing lamp. The chair is a locally crafted interpretation of European or Goanese design.

FARM FAMILY

Gopala Pillai and his wife, Saradakunjamma, live on a working farm in an eight-bedroom farmhouse that was built in 1922 in the village of Sasthamcotta, in the southern state of Kerala.

Tapioca, coconuts, jackfruit, and mangoes are grown on the property. The house, a traditional Kerala bungalow, designed and built by local craftsmen, is the largest in the area. Terraced verandas surround a central courtyard; the outbuildings include storehouses and a cowshed that boasts handcrafted wood stalls.

ABOVE: A welcome sign in English hangs above the front door, flanked by scenes from the life of Lord Krishna.

LEFT: Three generations of the Pillai family pose on the veranda.

RIGHT: The one-story farmhouse and its outbuildings, set in groves of coconuts, jackfruit, and mangoes, have clay-tiled roofs.

LEFT: A sewing machine has been set up in a room open to the interior courtyard, where women gathered when men met in an adjacent room. The columns have been painted in a naive trompe l'oeil wood-grain pattern.

LEFT: The front sitting room was used on more formal occasions and for political meetings. The canopy bed is reserved for special guests. The tall brass lamp burns coconut oil.

RIGHT: On the arcaded side veranda, the paneled teak shutters match the doors.

RIGHT: A graceful caned daybed set between two open doorways provides a cool resting spot to catch the breeze.

LEFT: The raised platform in the kitchen was used as additional seating at mealtimes. Several generations of family photographs form a frieze along the walls.

ABOVE: Outside the kitchen hangs an array of everyday objects, including a metal basket and a Malayalam calendar. The basket-shaped hat made of palm leaves is worn for working in the fields during the monsoon rains.

STATELY HOME

The Miranda house in Loutulim is one of Goa's most stately residences and has been in the same family since 1707. The Mirandas, descended from Hindu Brahmins, converted to Catholicism more than 200 years ago. The house's impressive oratory, or private chapel, underscores both the religious and decorative heritage of Goa as a Portuguese colony.

The coat of arms over the front door was presented to the family in 1871 by King Dom Luis of Portugal along with the title of Fidalgo Cavalheiro da Casa Real.

In the late 19th century, the appearance of the Colonial Baroque house underwent a dramatic transformation. Extensive alterations added cast-iron balconies, Italian tile and mosaic floors, and lattice-roofed verandas.

Mario Miranda, the current owner (his Italian name was chosen by his grandmother, an opera fan) and his wife, Habiba, now operate an art gallery in the second-floor ballroom.

ABOVE: A narrow sandy road leads from the small village, to the gates of the estate.

ABOVE: The facade is a contrast of stark white walls with black-painted cast-iron railings.

RIGHT: The trellised roof in one of the reception rooms not only allows air to circulate and filters light from small windows in the roof, but also creates complex shadows on the stenciled walls.

ABOVE FAR LEFT AND LEFT: The wide stone staircase was installed in the late 19th century. Nineteenth-century prints and reproductions of European Old Master paintings and drawings hang in the hall.

ABOVE: Italian tiles cover the floor of the reception room which extends nearly the full width of the house. The shuttered windows are framed in trompe l'oeil marble.

LEFT: A table set for tea stands before an Indo-Portuguese settee at one end of the long room.

ABOVE: The oratory is focused on an elaborately carved tiered altar that is inlaid with tile. In spite of the icons, reliquaries, and other religious objects, the private chapel, where the household worships daily, is in keeping with the decor of the rest of the house.

LEFT: The early 19th-century rosewood settee is one of a pair placed beneath the carved and gilded chair rail.

ABOVE: A reproduction of a Gauguin painting hangs between arched windows that look out over the interior courtyard.

LEFT: One of the large bedrooms is furnished with a graceful early 19th-century cane bed.

LEFT: Terra-cotta and black terrazzo - used for the bathtub, floor, and wainscoting - give the luxurious 1930s bathroom an almost ancient Roman look.

ABOVE: The Latin word salve, or welcome, has been worked in mosaic on the threshold of the master bedroom.

RIGHT: A majestic four-poster canopy bed dominates the master bedroom. The tile floor is decorated with a delicate pattern of flowers, birds, and dogs.

RIGHT: Anglo-Indian lounge chairs surround the desk in the red-walled study that adjoins the master bedroom. A Japanese ceramic jar holds rolls of paper. The windows are in the mid-19th-century Gothic Revival style.

ABOVE: The two verandas that
were added to the back of the
building in the late 19th century
are the most comfortable and
often-used spaces in the Miranda
house today. The doors on the
right lead to the oratory.

LEFT: In the large stone-floored kitchen at the back of the house, dried palm leaves are used to kindle the wood fire. The hole in the tiled roof, now a smoke vent, was originally made by the wild monkeys that live in the surrounding countryside.

RIGHT: Among the implements in the old-fashioned kitchen are food storage bottles and spices, large stone pestles and mortars, a small butcher's block, and utensils for scaling fish and hulling coconuts.

BOMBAY

MONUMENTAL MANSION

Set on Malabar Hill, one of the grandest sites in Bombay, Kilachand House is a 25-bedroom mansion that was built by a Parsi family in the late 1880s on a street known as the Street of Maharajas.

Tanil Kilachand, the present owner, was born in the house, which was bought from the maharaja of Patiala by his father, a commodity trader. In its heyday, more than a 100 people – including a staff of gardeners, carpenters, and housekeepers – lived in the house.

Nowadays, one of the only opportunities for Kilachand and his wife, Nilima, to entertain on a grand scale would be a family wedding. Then dinner would be served to 500, and as many as 2,000 might attend the reception.

ABOVE: The trees that line the wide street on Malabar Hill were once part of a dense forest.

LEFT: An Italianate marble urn is one of a pair on the steps of the mansion.

RIGHT: The present facade of the house, including two round turrets believed to be the zenana, or harem, was added in the 1920s.

ABOVE: At the back of the house, a wooden walkway links two wings of the residence.

RIGHT: Twin symmetrical marble staircases rise gracefully from the entrance hall.

ABOVE: A garden of bonsai adjoins the courtyard, which has a floor of Chinese glazed tiles.

RIGHT: On the second-floor gallery, the double wooden doors are inset with stained-glass panels.

FAR RIGHT: One of the main drawing rooms, which spans the entire width of the house, is furnished in a Western style with circular ottomans, Art Deco club sofas, formal family portraits, and a now rarely used grand piano. The marble-floored room, facing southeast, takes advantage of Bombay's cooling sea breezes. Ceiling fans help circulate the air.

ABOVE: The enormous dining room, with its Rococo plaster ceiling, is now used only on formal occasions. The table is set with silver *tahli* table settings.

RIGHT: Sterling silver serving pieces are crowded into a cabinet in the dining room.

LEFT: Outside the dining room, a small sink that replaces the traditional ewer and basin allows guests to rinse their hands before and after meals.

ABOVE: The billiard room, which has not been used in recent years, recalls the time when the mansion functioned as a club.

RED HOUSE

Shabda Samuel Koder and Gladys, his wife of 65 years, live in the distinctive house that has been in the Koder family since 1568.

Overlooking a leafy park, the house in Cochin - on the southwest of India's tropical Malabar Coast - stands on the road to the harbor.

An important figure in Cochin's Jewish community, which was established by expatriate Jews from Portugal in the 16th century, Koder is a prominent scholar, businessman, and a friend of viceroys and prime ministers.

The house has always been painted red. Its angled bays, white-painted casement windows, and blue trim, as well as its eclectic interior, combine Chinese, Portuguese, Dutch, and British architectural elements.

ABOVE: As on nearly every front door in Cochin, a small enamel plaque indicates the location of the property.

ABOVE LEFT: Huge shade trees line the road in front of the house.

LEFT: The three-bayed red facade of the house with its blue-and-white-painted details is as charming as it is distinctive.

ABOVE AND LEFT: Stairs lead to a landing with an unusual Chinese Chippendale banister. The white-painted cast-iron swan is one of a pair that decorates the entrance hall. Black-and-white glazed tiles on the steps are a dramatic accent.

ABOVE: The furniture in the spacious living room has been placed around the rug decorated with a large Star of David.

FAR LEFT: In the living room, a life-size portrait of Shabda Samuel Koder's father peers out from behind the Regency-style sofa.

LEFT: A plaster bust of Winston Churchill, family photographs, and cutouts of Mrs. Koder's mother and a friend in 1920s dresses stand on a whatnot in the living room.

LEFT: Old photographs of proudly won trophies as well as business associates are randomly piled up on a rattan chair in the sunroom off the dining room.

LEFT: Nearly two dozen family photographs of weddings, relatives, and friends crowd a small table in the dining room.

RIGHT: A gate closes off the stair on the top-floor landing. A carved screen with fabric panels shields a study area lined with bookshelves.

RIGHT: In the sparsely furnished dining room, a carved and pierced Burmese table and a pair of 19th-century Chinese Export chairs have been effectively placed in relation to the arched doorways that lead to the sun room.

JODHPUR

Rooms with a View

On the edge of the Thar or Great Indian Desert stands Jodhpur, the second largest city in Rajasthan. Dominated by a rocky promontory on which stands the fort, the city is a jumble of winding streets.

Inderraji Singhvi and his family live in a house built in the 19th century by his ancestor Dewan Merrajui Singhvi, a prime minister to Maharaja Mansinghjhi's court.

With its proximity to the fortress and its dramatic view over the city, the house continues to enjoy a prominent position in the community, as does the family that lives there.

ABOVE: The grand white house is hidden at the end of a narrow street.

LEFT: The rocky face of the cliff overshadows the inner courtyard of the house.

ABOVE RIGHT: The head of the family occupies the rooms above the main entrance.

ABOVE FAR RIGHT: Newly painted wall decorations in the traditional Jodhpur style surround the entrance gateway.

RIGHT: The series of buildings constructed or altered in successive periods is connected by an interior courtyard.

LEFT: During the summer, the family sleeps on iron beds on the roof.

BELOW LEFT: An enclosed balcony has been fitted with wooden shutters. The carved openwork screens called jalis afforded women a view of the front entrance while preserving their privacy.

RIGHT: A scalloped arch frames the white-painted stone steps that lead up to the second floor.

RIGHT CENTER: The traditional Hindu white plaster detailing contrasts with the colorful wall and door decorations.

FAR RIGHT: A window in the living room overlooks the old city.

BELOW RIGHT: A family photograph hangs on one of the columns in the living room.

BELOW RIGHT CENTER: In a corner of the living room stands an oval bathtub carved from a single block of marble.

FAR RIGHT: Both the front door and the ceiling boast ornate architectural woodwork.

LOUTULIM

PORTUGUESE BUNGALOW

The eldest of nine children, Rosa Costa Dias now lives – since her return to the subcontinent from Lisbon in 1967 – in her late father's house, built in 1874.

The bungalow, a hybrid of Eastern and Western styles, reflects the European presence in Goa since the Portuguese colonized the territory on India's west coast in the 16th century. Most of the furnishings are highly carved and ornamented in the Rococo and Victorian styles. The elaborate private chapel, unique in Goa, and the collection of Chinese Export porcelain are indicative of the enduring Portuguese influence in southern India.

ABOVE: A paved road passes through the tropical landscape.

LEFT: Rosa Costa Dias crochets on the front terrace of the house.

ABOVE RIGHT, RIGHT, AND FAR RIGHT: From a distance, only the Indian elements – the low-pitched tiled roof, wide veranda, and pastel colors – are visible. But the Gothic-style windows, cluster columns, and fretted spandrels typify the European heritage of the house.

ABOVE FAR RIGHT: Outside the door, a balcão, consisting of two concrete seats, was the traditional place to sit in the early evening.

ABOVE: Blue-and-white
Cantonese Export porcelain is on
display in the dining room.

RIGHT: The cut-glass chandelier
in the main reception room is still
lit with candles for weddings and
special family occasions.

ABOVE, ABOVE RIGHT, AND RIGHT: The shrine in the private chapel, established by two family priests, is a kaleidoscopic display of painted icons, ivory images of the Virgin and saints, European glass vases, late-19th-century Chinese porcelain, electrified candles, and gilded wood doors. The chapel is used for prayers every day at noon.

ABOVE, ABOVE LEFT, AND LEFT:
In the master bedroom, a
crocheted spread made by Dona
Costa Dias covers an ornate four-
poster bed, a local interpretation
of English art furniture of the
1880s. A Chinese plate and bowl
set in the washstand, a dressing
table, and a secretary are offset by
the plain plaster walls.

TOP: In one of the other bedrooms, a pair of wardrobes is carved with the traditional Indian vine motif.

ABOVE: For maximum ventilation, open wood partitions are the only separation between the rooms.

ABOVE: A hurricane-shaded candlestick and old books rest on the marble top of an Indian Victorian console table.

RIGHT: In an otherwise bare room, a Regency-inspired Indian sofa, made in Goa, and curtainless window pelmets create a dramatic effect under a carved wood ceiling.

ABOVE: Years of smoke and cooking have given the walls of the kitchen its charcoal patina. The coconut shells are stored to be used for fuel.

RIGHT: Near the kitchen, rice and tamarind are stored in unglazed earthenware jars.

ABOVE: Rice, grown in the property's paddy fields, is stored in the dirt-floored pantry. Bamboo ladders lean against the wall.

LEFT: The baskets are used for harvesting in the fields.

ONE OF A PAIR

Located in the Girgaum area, one of Bombay's oldest neighborhoods, the town house was built in 1909 as one of a matching pair and has always been occupied by members of the extended Kilachand family. It now belongs to the beneficiaries of the Kilachand Bevchand Trust.

The exterior masonry, cast-iron railings, and pointed arches, along with such interior details as mosaic floors and frescoed walls, have attained a rich patina.

ABOVE: The matching houses have arched porticoes topped with small terraces.

ABOVE LEFT: A hand-colored photograph, enclosed in a glass dome, stands on a cabinet in which are stored red-fabric-bound accounting books.

LEFT: The living room floor is a mosaic of bits of broken pottery and Chinese porcelain.

RIGHT: Bombay's humid climate has gradually peeled away layers of paint, giving the living room walls a mottled, ancient look.

HYDERABAD

ARTISTIC CENTER

Built in 1899 in the suburbs of Hyderabad, the house has always been a center for writers and artists. Dr. Hasanuddin Ahmed, a professor of literature whose grandfather built the house, is a member of the Nawayat family, a clan of Arab origin who came to India more than 600 years ago and settled on the western coast.

Now, six generations live on the estate, which includes outbuildings that once housed printing presses. The main residence is a curious vernacular mixture of Neoclassical and Gothic Revival styles.

On the exterior, pointed-arched openings flank an impressive Ionic-columned portico. In the interior, fretted windows, some with stained glass, and polished marble floors form a backdrop for a collection of Anglo-Indian Victorian heirlooms.

ABOVE: The suburban street outside the property is lined with ordinary modern buildings.

LEFT: Dr. Hasanuddin Ahmed often reads the morning paper on the wide veranda with its ocher-painted walls.

ABOVE: A double-walled arcade screens the house from the noises of the busy street.

LEFT AND BELOW: A long path leads ceremoniously up to the main entrance.

LEFT: The potted plants surrounding the shady garden room are a typically Indian feature. Printing presses once were operated in the outbuildings.

ABOVE: Portraits of distinguished family members hang in the high-ceilinged living room in the austere Muslim tradition.

ABOVE: The inlaid Aesthetic movement furniture, embellished with Minton tiles, is original.

ABOVE: A bookcase, filled with leather-bound books in Urdu and Persian written by distinguished members of the literary family, stands in the center of the hall.

ABOVE: Beneath the painted wood-beamed ceiling in the dining room, Gothic cabinets are set into the pink plaster walls.

ABOVE: Antique china is stored in a handsome 18th-century Gothic-style breakfront in the kitchen.

LEFT: A cut-glass hurricane lantern stands in front of one of the stained-glass windows in the dining room.

ABOVE: The copper-and-brass Turkish coffeepot is one of a pair displayed on carved-wood wall brackets in the dining room.

ABOVE RIGHT: The pairs of oil lamps, serving tables, and arched windows create a formal symmetry. The dining table and chairs were made locally.

RIGHT: Bamboo blinds shade a corner of the veranda, transforming it into a cool place to relax, work, or chitchat.

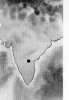

EDWARDIAN VILLA

Built at the very end of the 19th century, outside Hyderabad, the Edwardian villa now owned by Astad E. Chinoy was once part of a vast, secluded estate. Twenty gardeners maintained the extensive grounds, which boasted tennis courts and ponds. At night, jackals could be heard in the surrounding countryside, and even a small house party meant more than fifty guests.

Now, wisteria almost overwhelms the Italianate porte cochère, and paint peels from the weathered walls. Threatened by encroaching urban development, the grounds have been subdivided and the Chinoy house has the quality of a castle spellbound.

ABOVE: The present road that leads to the villa is a striking contrast to the old estate.

LEFT: Flowering quince, hibiscus, and oleander frame the Italianate villa. Its most striking exterior feature is three levels of wide, balustraded veranda.

RIGHT: A conservatory opens onto a raised terrace above the entrance, which is dotted with potted plants and covered with brilliant bougainvillea.

FAR LEFT: A game of solitaire is set up on a card table.

LEFT AND BELOW LEFT: Majolica jardinieres and green-and-white French rattan chairs and sofas transform the veranda into an informal year-round living room.

RIGHT: Two easy chairs with loosely fitted slipcovers stand like old dowagers in front of the rosewood and etched-glass windows of the drawing room.

ABOVE: Hats, umbrellas, walking sticks, and a cricket bat ornament the severe but elegant hatstand.

LEFT: The grand staircase rises at the center of the house. Tiled wainscoting lines the wall.

ABOVE: In the drawing room, the parquet floor of wood from Nepal has a herringbone border.

RIGHT: Etched-glass doors and a fretwork screen act as a prelude to the drawing room. A damask-covered pelmet divides the room.

RIGHT: The heavy draperies, fringed seating pieces upholstered in damask, and Napoleonic vitrines with Harrods labels are all of European lineage. Only the ceiling fan hints at the Indian location. The layout of the furniture has not changed since the house was built.

THE RURAL DWELLING

India is made of thousands of villages connected to one another by a dense and well-traveled network of roads. More than anything, it was variations of climate and geography that affected the highly individual architecture of India's rural dwellings. In Kutch, a great expanse of hard mud during the dry season and a virtual island during the monsoon, round houses made of mud brick and cow dung - and decorated with low geometric, often mirror-inlaid reliefs - are raised on platforms. These, along with interior ledges on which the furniture is arranged provide protection from flooding. In the tropical south, houses made from woven palm fronds offer shelter both from the frequent rainstorms and hot sun. In these and nearly all other rural dwellings, no matter how humble, there is a shared pride in which the mundane elements of everyday life - medicine bottles, tin cans, and cooking utensils - are all proudly and artfully arranged to become essential components of a colorful and decorative environment.

LEFT: Girls in Hodka wear armfuls of bangles and strong colored fabrics.

ABOVE: A family stands on the roof of their house in Ladakh.

HODKA

Village Life

Political turmoil between India and Pakistan, inaccessible roads, and interminable droughts have had a serious impact on villages like Hodka, in the northern state of Kutch. Only recently have some inquisitive Western travelers discovered the isolated area near the Pakistan border.

About 30 families belonging to the Harijan community live in the village. Their traditional livelihood was cattle raising, but recently the community has earned a reputation for its fine handicrafts, particularly mirrored embroidery and leatherwork.

In response to the harsh natural landscape, the women of Kutch transform their barren settings into colorful and imaginative environments – with mirror-bedecked garments and colorfully painted rooms, as well as the intricate-patterned mudwork for which Kutch is renowned.

ABOVE: Tire tracks mark the way to Hodka village, a settlement nearly hidden among prickly bawal bushes.

LEFT: All the houses in the village have either terra-cotta - tiled or thatched roofs.

RIGHT: Children play in an indola, or wood baby cradle, decorated with bits of mirror set into the frame.

ABOVE: A painted stylized plant design outlines the doorway of one of the village houses.

LEFT: Inside one house, the walls are covered with a whitewashed pattern of mud and cow dung.

BELOW LEFT: In a traditional round house, a stack of bedsheets or quilts is flanked by a sangira, or food cupboard, on the left, and a kothar, or grain chest.

BELOW: Stylized peacock and flower motifs have been scratched into the blue-painted surface of a weathered metal door.

ABOVE: The door to each house in the village is different. This one, to a round house, is of wood, with metal cross braces and studs.

RIGHT: Inside the round house, a double row of meticulously arranged brass dishes hangs above the crenelated wainscoting.

RIGHT: A bold use of color and pattern links the small window to the shelves in one of the houses. Even everyday objects become part of the overall decoration.

BELOW: A leather bag hangs from a peg near a wooden door.

ABOVE: Hand-operated sewing machines are stored near a pile of quilts made in the village and meant for sale in Delhi and Bombay. The patchwork is done by machine, the quilting by hand.

ABOVE: Skeins of undyed wool, called chado, which will be woven into blankets, hang from the rafters of one of the houses.

ABOVE: On the roof of one of the houses, made from a local grass called drabha, is a collection of mundane objects, including an empty gasoline can, a fabric-bound ring worn on the head to balance a water jar, a pair of leather sandals, and a spool, or cherokhi, used for winding thread.

ABOVE: Plates and jars, meant for serving bread, dhal, and buttermilk, are made in the nearby Lodai village using a technique where several layers of colored slip are scratched with a pattern.

ABOVE: In one of the houses, a wall of storage is immaculately arranged. A patchwork quilt covers a stack of dowry bedsheets. The women use only their hands to mold mud and cow dung into bold relief patterns, which they finish with whitewash.

ABOVE: A pile of forty or fifty bedsheets is covered with a cloth and flanked by the neatly stored possessions that belong to one of the village families. Each girl is expected to make her own dowry of at least 15 sheets - used for sleeping on the floor - by the time she is about 18 years old.

STONE HOUSE

The road that leads from Srinagar to Leh passes Sonamarg, a remote village that is over 17,000 feet above sea level.

Muhammed Hadi, son of Haji Abbas, a farmer, lives with his extended family in one of a group of about fifteen stone houses. Although the house was built in 1983, its plan and the mud and stone materials used in its construction reflect centuries-old local traditions.

ABOVE: Members of the extended family sit on the small balcony.

TOP LEFT: A small group of stone houses clusters on the hillside beside the river Sind, which is fed by melting snow from the peaks.

ABOVE LEFT: Blue dots frame the windows of the second floor, where four rooms are occupied by the family.

LEFT: The front room is enlivened by vibrant blue-green - painted walls. The house has electricity and a battery-operated stereo, but no running water.

RIGHT: The kitchen has only a seven-foot ceiling and a minimum of decoration. The smoke-blackened wood beams, like the shelf above the wood-fueled cooking stove, are decorated with blue-green dots.

LEH

TOURIST ATTRACTION

The stone-and-clay house that belongs to the Kiddar family is located in the center of the remote town of Leh, 11,500 feet above sea level. Once inaccessible, the ancient town has in the past few years attracted increasing numbers of tourists.

In addition to visiting Leh's historic Likir monastery and a dramatic fortified palace, some intrepid travelers find their way to the Kiddar house to see its exceptional kitchen – an immaculate room lined with rows of gleaming brass and aluminum teapots and cookware.

ABOVE: The owner's wife looks out a window of the Kiddar house.

TOP LEFT: Leh is surrounded by mountain peaks. A gilded pinnacle crowns the roof of the Buddhist monastery.

ABOVE CENTER LEFT: Alfalfa, dried and stored on the flat roof of the house, also provides insulation. The stone walls are whitewashed.

LEFT AND RIGHT: Old brass and copper pots are displayed on shelves in the kitchen, where the family spends four months a year. Turned-wood columns support the beamed ceiling. Wood or dung is burned in the cast-iron stove decorated with brass openwork.

200

LEFT: Members of the family sit on carpeted platforms to eat from a series of colorfully painted tables.

BELOW LEFT: In the Chotkang, or prayer room, deities are kept behind the glass doors of the richly decorated shrine.

RIGHT: Graduated brass ladles and brass-bound butter churns hang near other metal vessels, all used for making gurgur, the traditional butter tea. Some local women drink as many as 100 cups of the tea a day.

COLORFUL COLLAGE

Within the walls of the fortress of Jaisalmer winds a narrow street lined with organic-shaped stone dwellings. Raman Singh Solanki and his family live in a small multilevel house.

The exterior is freshly painted every year in orange and white; the interior is a multicolor collage of folk art and family mementos.

ABOVE AND RIGHT: White-painted steps lead to the front door of the house. The small balcony is a vantage point for a view of the street below.

LEFT: In the inner courtyard of the house, stone steps allow access to the flat roof.

ABOVE: Family photographs and
religious images are displayed
behind glass and embedded in the
plaster wall. Wooden battens
conceal the very recently added
electric wires.

ABOVE: Highly polished brass
cooking vessels are displayed on
plaster-and-wood shelves above
a frieze of mirror fragments.

ABOVE: Old light bulbs are strung along the ceiling as decoration. The wall near the sleeping area is covered with framed deities and a collage of mirror fragments.

ABOVE: The double niche in the kitchen includes a tiny window, a small brazier for cooking, and a sparkling collection of polished-brass double-boilers.

FLOATING HOME

During most of his life, Golam Rasool, now in his seventies, has lived on a houseboat. His home for the past ten years has been a small boat, called a *dunga*, that is permanently moored on Dal Lake in Srinagar, Kashmir.

Living on a lake is one of the cheapest housing solutions in India – the purchase price and the annual mooring fee are the occupant's only expenses.

But today few young people, no matter how poor, opt for this floating lifestyle, rejecting it as old-fashioned and demeaning. For Rasool, it is a comfortable way of life that also provides a closeness with nature, pleasant even when the lake ices up as it sometimes does in winter.

ABOVE AND LEFT: The dunga *boat is moored near the shore of Dal Lake, floating on a sea of green weeds. Sections of the roof can be propped open to enhance the circulation of air.*

TOP: Golam Rasool, a Muslim, smokes his hookah in the main living area. A small basket contains hot coals, used for the pipe. The room is ornamented with a painting on velvet of the Great Wall of China and a brass-and-enamel plaque with religious inscriptions.

ABOVE: In the kitchen, a loose electric cable snakes from the power line on the roof to a small terra-cotta stove. Most of the cooking is done on the shore. Sliding shutters open for air and views. Adhesive vinyl partially covers the walls.

ABOVE: Neatly stacked tin trunks contain clothing and valuables. The large terra-cotta pot holds fresh water drawn from a tap 100 yards away on the lakeshore.

ABOVE: Bedrolls are unfolded at night when the occupants of the boat sleep on a cedar-plank floor worn smooth by use.

HODKA

Round House

Bungas, or round huts, have for centuries been a traditional form of housing in the Kutch area of the Thar Desert in Gujarat.

The round shape exposes less surface to the elements and so minimizes damage from the hot sun, cold winds, and sandstorms. To protect them from flooding during the three-month-long monsoons, the structures are also raised on mud platforms.

Rai Shi Jumma Abrahim and his family own a small group of huts built in a single day in 1982 by men of the nearby Wadha community from a combination of wood, mud, clay, and concrete. Twenty people now live in the cluster of houses. Inside, colored traditional geometric patterns adorn the walls, textiles, and spectacular conical bamboo roofs.

ABOVE: Cattle breeding is the main livelihood of the region.

LEFT: The group of huts owned by the Abrahim family is on a mud terrace surrounded by tall grasses and prickly bawal *bushes.*

TOP RIGHT: The roofs of the round houses are lined with plastic sheeting and thatched.

ABOVE RIGHT: Women and girls from a nearby village use their heads to carry vessels of water, which they fetch at sunset from the nearby well.

213

LEFT: In the main hut, the traditional wall decorations were painted by craftsmen from the Wadha community. Bars on the small window are for security.

RIGHT: On the inside of the roof, bamboo slats have been bound together and painted in a decorative geometric pattern.

BELOW RIGHT: Dowry bedsheets are stacked on turned-wood stools and concealed behind printed textiles. The painted tin trunks are used for storage.

RIGHT: The main hut is centered on a charpoy, the traditional Indian bed strung with rope, reserved for the head of the household, whose wife and children sleep next to him on bedrolls on the floor.

TYPICAL FARMHOUSE

Situated in the sandy dry landscape of Rajasthan near the town of Bissau, the farmhouse owned by Chokharam Chaudhury is typical of the area.

Enclosed by a fence of tangled, thorny brush, the small complex of buildings constructed from a mixture of mud and dung blends easily into the natural landscape. The family keeps goats, sheep, camels, cows, and buffaloes, and grows millet, *gunwar,* and lentils in the fertile season following the monsoon rains.

ABOVE: The arid landscape of the Thar Desert is dotted with trees.

ABOVE LEFT: A well provides the Chaudhury family with fresh water.

LEFT: The thatched-roof dwellings provide living spaces for all the members of the extended family.

RIGHT: Sculpted mud walls divide the yard for domestic activities.

ABOVE: A small metal enclosure functions as a cool place to store food or as a cage to protect small animals.

ABOVE LEFT: On the mud-brick wall hang three torans, small, flat wood and metal artifacts, each marking the marriage of a daughter. Parrots are considered symbolic messengers of love.

LEFT: The palm impressions beside the entrance indicate the births of two sons. Women wear the silver-embroidered fabric hanging on the door every day, even when they work in the fields.

RIGHT: The mud walls are renewed at festival times each year. The pottery jars are for carrying and storing water.

PALM LEAF ABODE

The palm tree is a familiar sight in the south of India, and palm fronds are the most popular building material in the villages around Cochin. Having purchased a small piece of land with their life savings, the Jose family – a mother, son, and daughter-in-law – constructed a tiny two-room house out of woven palm, bought in a nearby village.

ABOVE: Tall palm trees dwarf the tiny houses in Cochin.

LEFT: A window is set into the wall of palm leaves. The decorative pattern of braided leaves helps keep out the rain.

RIGHT: A fence encloses the house, which stands in an immaculately kept sandy yard. The Jose family are the proud owners of three palm trees that came with their land.

LEFT: A photograph of the owner's mother rests on a ledge.

LEFT: A partition of palm leaves with a clerestory opening separates the two interior rooms. A bedroll hangs on the wall.

RIGHT: Religious objects assembled on a small wooden shelf include a Perpetual Light, an image of Saint Anthony, a statuette of the Virgin Mary, and the deity Verlankani - an example of the casual crossing of religious borders that often happens in India, one faith absorbing the deities of another.

RIGHT: Cooking utensils hang in the area used for preparing meals. There is no electricity, and water is brought in from a public tap down the road.

Decorated Village

In the Great Indian Desert, near the border of Pakistan, a few miles from the walled city of Jaisalmer, are some of the most strikingly decorated houses in Rajasthan.

In villages like Baramsar and Roopsi, there is almost no rain and even clouds are rare. During the droughts, water must be brought in by camel cart from Jaisalmer. Particularly noteworthy is the local traditional decoration - distinctive white freehand designs on ocher-colored walls.

ABOVE: The family of Deendyan Jain stands outside their house in the village of Baramsar.

LEFT AND RIGHT: Various facades in the villages of Baramsar and Roopsi display a range of flat, stylized, and geometric designs, often with bird and camel motifs.

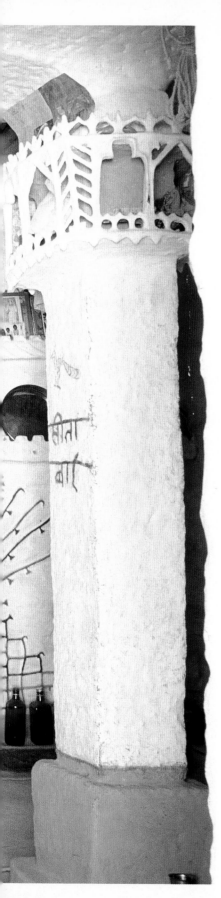

ABOVE: In Deendyan Jain's house in Baramsar, the room used for cooking has a small stove in one corner and a built-in cupboard for storing food.

LEFT: The main room of Pratab Singh's house in Roopsi features a spectacular floor-to-ceiling array of shelves made from papier-mâché and clay. Both mundane and special objects are carefully grouped in separate niches and arranged around a deity that occupies the central compartment.

RIGHT: Terra-cotta tiles surround a niche in a house in Baramsar. Most of the houses in the village are equipped with electricity. The cassette player is a modern Western amenity, although the music played is usually Indian.

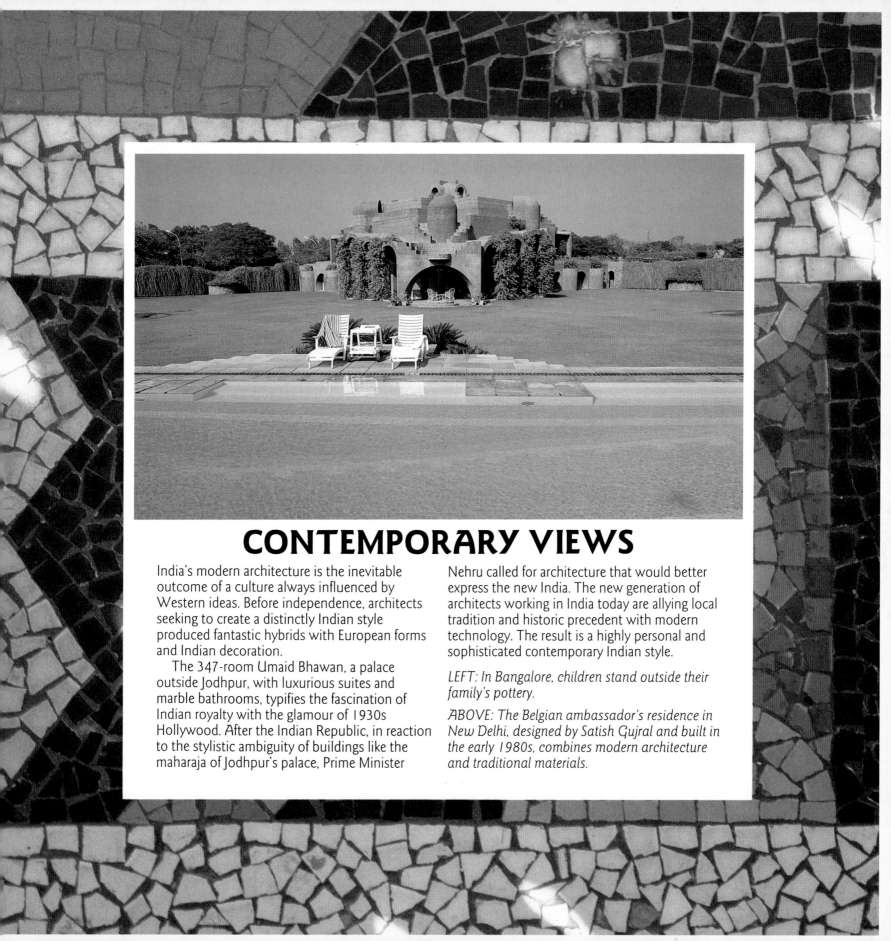

CONTEMPORARY VIEWS

India's modern architecture is the inevitable outcome of a culture always influenced by Western ideas. Before independence, architects seeking to create a distinctly Indian style produced fantastic hybrids with European forms and Indian decoration.

The 347-room Umaid Bhawan, a palace outside Jodhpur, with luxurious suites and marble bathrooms, typifies the fascination of Indian royalty with the glamour of 1930s Hollywood. After the Indian Republic, in reaction to the stylistic ambiguity of buildings like the maharaja of Jodhpur's palace, Prime Minister Nehru called for architecture that would better express the new India. The new generation of architects working in India today are allying local tradition and historic precedent with modern technology. The result is a highly personal and sophisticated contemporary Indian style.

LEFT: In Bangalore, children stand outside their family's pottery.

ABOVE: The Belgian ambassador's residence in New Delhi, designed by Satish Gujral and built in the early 1980s, combines modern architecture and traditional materials.

Art Deco Luxury

In 1928, the Maharaja Umaid Singh began to construct an immense palace known as Umaid Bhawan outside Jodhpur. Designed by an English establishment architect, Edward Vaughn Lancaster, but not finished until 1943, just a few years before the end of the Raj, the marble and red sandstone complex of 347 rooms was the last of the opulent Indian royal palaces. The ambitious building synthesized the Art Deco style with the romance of Old India. S. Norblin, a Polish artist, coordinated the decoration.

The palace, which took 13 years to complete, was started as a public works program during a famine. At one time more than 3,000 people worked on the 3¹/₂-acre building. About 12 miles of railroad were constructed to bring the sandstone from the nearest quarry.

The materials were local, but the palace's stylistic inspiration derives from the Victoria Memorial in Calcutta, which in turn derives from the Taj Mahal. The palace is now a luxury hotel, with the present maharaja, Gaj Singh II, occupying a private wing.

ABOVE: On one of the terraces, water drips slowly through a lattice of branches.

ABOVE FAR LEFT: With its towers and domes, the palace stands dramatically on a hill.

FAR LEFT: In one of the suites, the velvet club chairs and the sectional sofa are Art Deco.

ABOVE: The pale pink and black bedroom that once belonged to the Maharani Badan Kanwar reflects the occupant's sophisticated taste.

ABOVE: The wall sconces that flank the shower were innovations in India when they were first installed in the 1930s.

LEFT: The maharani's bathroom is entirely clad in highly patterned gray marble. The bathtub was carved from a single block of rose onyx.

ABOVE: The marble-and-onyx sink is set in front of a mirrored niche.

ABOVE: The seating in Maharaja Umaid Singh's formal sitting room is covered in leopard-skin fabric. Most of the pieces were reproduced by local craftsmen from books and catalogues when the original shipment was lost en route from Maple's in London.

RIGHT: Norblin painted the murals in the sitting room, including the one that depicts a wild boar hunt. The chrome-and-marquetry table lamp is Art Deco.

ABOVE: The color of the velvet-upholstered living room furniture was carefully coordinated to match the exotic woodwork.

LEFT: Even the stainless-steel water pitcher and streamlined wall switch for the ceiling fans are in the style of the period.

ABOVE: The Ruhlmann-style bed in the maharaja's bedroom is decorated with his personal emblem. A pair of lacquer screens and spiral lamps by the French designer Jean-Michel Frank create a geometric symmetry.

RIGHT: In the sitting area of the bedroom, the curved lacquer-and-chrome coffee table and orange-stain - upholstered suite contrast with the rectilinear shape of the room. In Jodhpur's winters, a fireplace was a welcome feature.

AHMEDABAD

MODERN CLASSIC

In the early 1950s, at about the same time he undertook his large-scale public commissions at Chandigarh, the Swiss architect Le Corbusier was asked to design a number of private homes in Ahmedabad.

Set in a large park, in an area called Shahibag, the cast-concrete and brick house is skillfully integrated into its environment. A collection of modules is connected at different levels so that the roof of one becomes the grassed terrace of another.

Floor-to-ceiling pivoting doors provide a dynamic interplay between the interior and the exterior spaces.

ABOVE: A concrete slide takes bathers from the roof into the pool.

ABOVE LEFT: A gardener mows the grass on the roof terrace.

LEFT: In the tiled barrel-vaulted entrance, a large paper Japanese lantern illuminates an antique Indian brass dowry chest.

RIGHT: The interior is a bold synthesis of traditional Indian elements and modern Western design. Pivoting doors open all the rooms to the garden; low rosewood-and-cane divans complement the slate floor.

REFINED COLLECTION

Traditional Indian crafts have been Pupul Jayakar's lifelong passion. For over 20 years, Jayakar, who was a close friend of Indira Gandhi and chairman of the Festival of India, has been instrumental in the promotion and development of Indian handicrafts.

Now in her seventies, Jayakar has since 1981 lived in a 1930s bungalow in one of New Delhi's most prestigious neighborhoods. There, she has assembled in a spare Japanese-inspired environment her eclectic and refined collection of favorite folk-art objects.

ABOVE: A wide circular driveway leads up to the house and its surrounding gardens.

LEFT: An enormous antique clay pot stands near the door.

RIGHT: In the living room, Victorian furniture, upholstered in red velvet and raw silk, creates a bold contrast with the Japanese-inspired wall panel and huge paper lamp.

LEFT: The Indian rattan stool, silk-covered chairs, off-white walls, and woven straw from the northeast of India are all in the same hue.

RIGHT: Seashell fossils and a votive hand are carefully arranged on a marble platter in front of the two-seat button-back loveseat.

LEFT: Cane-back chairs, inlaid with mother-of-pearl, furnish the dining room. On the wall hangs a series of Madhubani paintings.

RIGHT: At the end of the small kitchen at the back of the house, a tall English-style glass-fronted cupboard spans the entire wall.

Renovated Haveli

The fortresslike *haveli*, built in 1776 outside of New Delhi, had been abandoned for 50 years. But enough of its noble architecture, a synthesis of Hindu and Islamic styles, remained for art historians Francis Wacziarg and Aman Nath to undertake an ambitious restoration project.

Over the course of two years, their efforts transformed a historic ruin into a vital contemporary environment. Although Wacziarg and Nath left the facade and most of the exterior unaltered, they had interior rooms and courtyards freshly painted and renovated.

Forty-six windows were opened to views of the surrounding landscape and new plumbing and electricity were installed.

The result of the restorers' careful attention to detail is a romantic refuge that succeeds in preserving its past while accommodating modern needs.

ABOVE: A small boy passes the entrance to the haveli.

LEFT: At sunset, the view of the house is magical.

RIGHT: Except for the modern cars, the water pump, and telephone poles, the landscape and scenes of local life around the haveli *have changed very little in the intervening centuries.*

ABOVE: Arches in an ancient Hindu form frame the courtyard.

RIGHT: The antique brass-studded doors contrast with the appliquéd window shades and tablecloth, which were made by Kirtu Bhandari.

FAR RIGHT: An ancient stone column base acts as a step for the raised shuttered door to the narrow veranda.

ABOVE: Oil lamps and a 19th-century stone carving of a bull fill a deep arched window recess.

LEFT: To celebrate the festival of Laksmi, the courtyard is transformed by candlelight into a romantic spectacle.

LEFT: The antique low folding chairs on the open veranda are from Shekahavati and were once used by women when they churned butter.

RIGHT: In the dining room, a takht, or high bed, has been converted into a table by raising it on stone drums.

ABOVE: Traditional pieces, including a low cot and an ironbound dowry chest, are the sole furnishings of a room off the central courtyard.

ABOVE: The simply appointed
bedroom, with traditional lime-
washed walls and charpoy, is a
serene retreat.

ARTISTS' RETREAT

The owners of the house in Shahibag, a suburb of Ahmedabad, have devoted many years to developing Indian crafts and skills and interpreting them for a sophisticated market.

With traditional Indian weaving skills as a starting point, the couple have developed a collection of original contemporary textiles and are currently working with such fashion designers as the Japanese Issey Miyake.

The couple's house acts as a showcase for their modern art, and a working haven for their artist friends. David Hockney, Richard Smith, and Howard Hodgkin are three of the artists of international stature who have lived on the estate. Inspired by the colors and traditions of Indian craftsmanship, they have experimented with such media as papermaking, printing, and weaving.

ABOVE: A group of local women in brightly colored saris, pass in front of the house.

LEFT: Traditional antique bronze urns dot the long veranda. Wicker shades and ceiling fans help keep the outdoor space cool.

RIGHT: White doves roam freely near the lily pond on the property.

LEFT: The spacious living room is simply furnished with three takhts, a bentwood rocker, and a round marble coffee table. The artworks are by visiting artists who came to learn about Indian techniques. The seating and pillows are covered in Indian woven fabrics. African Gray parrots live in graceful cages.

ABOVE: A kitelike sculpture by the English artist Richard Smith hangs high on the wall by a Japanese paper lantern.

ABOVE: The high-ceilinged bedroom, with its American quilt, Japanese lighting fixtures, American Eames lounge chair, and English Victorian chaise, presents an international and eclectic mix. Only the family photographs – which along with a representation of a deity hang above an eternal flame – as well as the ceiling fan and mosquito netting on the canopy bed hint at the Eastern locale.

ABOVE: In the sparse blue-and-white bathroom, a trompe l'oeil window of mosaic tiles decorates the wall. The shower curtain, with an appropriate gentle rainfall pattern, can be stretched across the room.

Masterful Brickwork

Laurie Baker, an English architect and housing consultant, has worked in India for 30 years. Since he had always lived in the mountains, he intentionally chose a hilly building site when he moved to Trivandrum in 1969 with his wife, Elizabeth.

For his low-income housing projects, Baker preferred to use brick, rather than concrete, since it required no finishing or maintenance. His own house, a series of multilevel structures that climb the hill, is made of brick manufactured nearby.

Working closely with local builders, the architect used an inventive combination of curved surfaces and planes, developing his ideas and plans on site rather than on paper. The result is a sensible and spontaneous-looking house – a witty example of imaginative problem-solving.

ABOVE: Coconut palms and banana trees line the dirt road opposite the entrance.

LEFT: Dogs are kept in the small enclosure above the gatehouse.

TOP: The painted iron gate is made up of amusing sculptural elements that recall tools and mechanical parts.

ABOVE: Potted plants fill the terrace garden that boasts a distant view of Mount Agaustya and the Western Ghats.

TOP: The sitting area near the kitchen is shaded by a roof tiled in the traditional pattern.

ABOVE: The walls of the living room are of exposed brick.

LEFT: Near the kitchen, a wood stove, retained in case of emergency, houses cooking utensils and coconuts.

ABOVE: The kitchen, with jackwood ceiling and black-oxide cement floor, is organized around a central gas cooking and food preparation island.

ABOVE: A compass and ivory scale ruler are architect's tools.

LEFT: The master bedroom doubles as a work area for both Laurie Baker and his wife, Elizabeth. The ceiling is intentionally unfinished. Because of the tropical climate, the end wall is made up of open wood slats that allow for the passage of air. The locally made floor tiles have been waxed to a high polish.

LEFT BELOW: A low seating unit nearly fills the small sitting room near the bedroom. Bits and pieces of pottery have been set into the brickwork.

RIGHT: The guest bedroom on the top floor is open to the elements. Mosquito netting is draped over the bed frames.

BELOW: The brickwork in the bedroom is both decorative and functional; the artistically shaped openings serve as air vents.

CULTURAL PRESERVATION

Francis Wacziarg, a French historian and former diplomat, has lived in India for the past 18 years. In his modern apartment in Nizamuddin, a suburb of New Delhi, Wacziarg has accumulated an enviable collection of Indian crafts and art objects.

The apartment in an early 1950s building acts as an unobtrusive backdrop for the unusual collection, which is a logical extension of the owner's interest in the preservation of the culture of Rajasthan.

ABOVE: Terra-cotta pots form a pyramid on the rooftop terrace.

ABOVE LEFT: The apartment is on the top floor of a 1950s building surrounded by greenery.

LEFT: All the furniture on the veranda came from Goa. The terra-cotta tile relief was commissioned by Francis Wacziarg and made in the small village of Molela.

ABOVE: A long corridor runs from the front door to the brightly lit bedroom. A papier-mâché turban box is used as a small Anglo-Indian table. A raja had the giant hookah made especially for his daughter's wedding.

LEFT: In the master bedroom, the 19th-century painting is of Laksmi, the Hindu goddess of wealth and beauty. The small marble statuette of a musician is from Jodhpur. The writing table is Anglo-Indian; the chair, from Goa, is an Indo-Portuguese version of Rococo.

FAR LEFT: A 19th-century painted-wood figure of a Buddhist monk, one of a pair that came from a palace in Calcutta, has been converted into a lamp and now presides over a collection of brass Rajasthani inkwells.

CENTER LEFT: The carved wood horse with seven heads is an unusual representation of the seven horses associated with Surya, the sun god.

LEFT: A rare 19th-century swimming baby Krishna in terra cotta from Rajasthan is displayed on an engraved brass dowry chest from Shekhavati.

BELOW FAR LEFT: The low 19th-century accountant's desk from western India was purchased in Jodhpur. It is topped with a miniature almirah, a cupboard, with delicate ivory columns.

BELOW CENTER LEFT: A Chinese painting on glass of the Peshwa dignitary Nana Phadnavis hangs above three polychrome figurines of soldiers made in Lucknow.

BELOW LEFT: The brass head of the Shiva deity covered the lingam, a phallic symbol, when it was not being worshiped. The cabinet, from Jodhpur, is rare; few pieces of furniture were used in traditional Indian interiors.

RIGHT: The turn-of-the-century royal portrait, the 150-year-old carved wood chairs that were part of a dowry in Shekhavati, the two-tier, star-shaped lacquer table from Bikaner, and the brass spoons that came from monasteries in Ladakh exemplify the varied artistry of Indian heritage celebrated in the interior.

LEFT: An 18th-century wood sculpture of the four-armed Vishnu, the preserver of the universe, comes from Gujarat.

RIGHT: The painting on glass of a princess, in the Chinese style, was done in India in the 19th century.

AHMEDABAD

TRADITIONAL REINTERPRETATION

When Amit Ambalal, a well-known contemporary artist, decided to build a studio in Ahmedabad, he sought to create a peaceful and relaxing environment where he and his friends could gather to work and socialize.

Although Ambalal and his wife, Raksha, had lived since 1971 in a concrete-and-steel house, they chose to approach the studio in a different way. The new building, designed by Sudhir Shah, was to be made of wood, following a traditional plan around a courtyard. The studio's focal point was to be Ambalal's collection of antique architectural elements – including sculptures, pillars, and doors from houses and temples. The architect and the artist were joined by a carpenter with more than 50 years of experience in traditional building methods. They worked daily according to a flexible plan to produce an innovative multilevel structure that links the past to the present.

ABOVE: An antique carving of a sleeping lion came from an ancient temple.

LEFT: The colonnade of the raised veranda came from Ahmedabad.

RIGHT: The tiled-roof house is an assemblage of spaces on different levels that encloses a courtyard.

275

LEFT: Traditional low seating, such as the divans with pillows and bolsters on one of the verandas, has been used throughout the studio.

RIGHT: The painting of Krishna on glass, set in a niche ornamented with carved woodwork, belonged to Amit Ambalal's grandfather.

ABOVE: A swing, typical of houses in Gujarat, has been installed on the terrace to take advantage of the garden view.

ABOVE: The modern chairs, designed by Amit Ambalal, with woven jute seats and backs and metal frames, give the study a light, open feeling.

OCTAGONAL BEACH HOUSE

Set on an extraordinary promontory in Trivandrum at the southernmost tip of the country, the octagonal beach house overlooks the Arabian Sea.

Built in 1984 by Klaus Schleusener, a German professor who has traveled widely throughout India, the house at Pulinkudi Cove was designed as an ideal vacation retreat.

Natural stone, terra-cotta tile, whitewashed granite, and recycled wood beams combine to create a simple second home.

ABOVE: The octagonal house is set on a hill on three acres of land facing the sea.

LEFT: A forest of palm trees adjoins a sandy beach at Pulinkudi Cove.

ABOVE RIGHT: The terrace is perched directly above the beach. Carved granite capitals are used as small side tables.

RIGHT: The living room is completely open to the view and the ocean breezes.

SHELTERING EAVES

In 1978, Adoor Gopalakrishnan built a house in the hills near Trivandrum, the City of the Sacred Snake and the capital of the state of Kerala.

Although Gopalakrishnan, one of India's foremost young film directors, used elements from a 200-year-old house that was being demolished and sold for firewood, his traditionally designed building is a contemporary statement with strong references to traditional Brahmin architecture.

The high-pitched roof and sheltering eaves protect from both the hot sun and the monsoons and are the one-level house's most salient features. Exposed rafters, tile floors, and bare brick and masonry walls give the stark interior a sense of drama.

*ABOVE AND ABOVE LEFT:
A graveled drive, patterned with
the shadows of palm fronds, leads
from the front gate to the house.*

*LEFT: The generous overhangs of
the tiled roof not only shelter a
veranda but also form a carport.*

ABOVE: Adoor Gopalakrishnan
sits on a covered porch, a modern
version of the poomukham, or
sacred front, where the
homeowner greeted his visitors.

ABOVE: A reproduction of the
Mona Lisa *hangs in the atrium,*
where a central font is open to the
sky and the tropical rains.

ABOVE: The film director's
numerous awards fill a bookshelf in
the lofty library and screening room.

TOP: Jackfruit and bananas flourish in the garden.

ABOVE: Vibrantly colored embroidered panels strike a note of color in the pristine kitchen.

RIGHT: Baskets filled with tamarinds, coconuts, jackfruit, pepper, and papayas, all grown on the property, await preparation in the pantry adjoining the kitchen.

LEFT: At the end of every typical Indian meal, whether at home or in a restaurant or large international hotel, paan is the final course. Consisting of a variety of ingredients often wrapped in a betel leaf, it is considered the essential digestive. In the north of India even the making of paan is considered a ceremonial ritual. The housewife will settle down with her small paan daan, sometimes made of wrought iron or brass, which will probably contain a supply of betel leaves, betel nuts, cardomoms and cloves, lime paste, catechu scented tobacco, and sometimes coconut.

The ingredients and the quality vary from state to state, and the connoisseur might refuse anything but Benarasi Paan.

Once the ingredients have been prepared and placed on the leaf, it is folded into a small triangle, and may be held together with a clove, or finished with silver leaf.

INDIAN BAZAAR

Belinda Richards

Many English words are recognized as Indian or Indian derivatives that came into the language during the Raj, the period of British rule in India.

BAZAAR

Indian and Middle Eastern term for a marketplace or a group of shops; in the West it refers to a charity sale of trinkets and other items.

JODHPURS

Riding breeches that fit close to the leg from the knee to the ankle and are worn with a low boot. They are modeled after similar trousers worn in Jodhpur in Rajasthan.

KHAKI

An adjective meaning dusty or dust-colored that comes from the Persian *khak*. In English, a brownish-yellow cotton cloth used for uniforms. Worn by some of the Punjab regiments at the Siege of Delhi; common in the British army generally during the campaigns of 1857-58, and subsequently in the American army.

POLO

The game of hockey on horseback originated in Persia, was played in the extreme west of the Himalayas until it was adopted in Calcutta around 1864, and quickly spread throughout the lower provinces and to Kashmir, where summer visitors took it up. It was first played in England in July 1871 and was transferred from there to the United States.

MOGUL

A magnate or important person. The word comes from the Persian *mughul*, or Mongol. An Indian Muslim descended from one of several conquering groups of Mongol, Turkish, and Persian origins.

PAJAMAS

"Leg clothing" in Hindi. A pair of loose trousers tied at the waist. Such clothing is worn by many people in India, including women of various classes, by Sikh men, and by most Muslims of both sexes.

JUGGERNAUT

A tremendous force. The word is derived from the Hindu god Jagannath, Lord of the Universe, a name of Krishna, worshiped as Vishnu at the shrine of Puri in Orissa. The image, an amorphous idol, is annually taken in procession on a huge cart.

PUNDIT

A scholar or man of knowledge, from the Hindi *pandit*. Strictly, it refers to a man learned in Sanskrit lore.

DELICACIES

AMCHOOR
Dried raw mango, in powder or in slices, used in North Indian dishes to add a tangy zest to meat, fish, or vegetables, much as Westerners use lemon.

CHILI
The pod of the red pepper (*Capiscum*). The plant came to India from South America.

CHUTNEY
A spicy relish often made from mangoes, chili peppers, or tomatoes. The word comes from the Hindi *catni*, but it was more often eaten by Muslims.

CURRY
A spicy dish of meat, fish, or vegetables, cooked with a quantity of ground spices, red pepper, and turmeric.

DHAL
Dried split peas and other dried beans that are a mainstay of Indian cuisine.

GHEE
Clarified butter used for cooking, which does not need refrigeration. Used universally throughout India, instead of oil or other fats.

GURGUR
Tea with butter added to it, consumed in great quantities, in small cups, in the area of Ladakh and northern India.

KEDGEREE
In English a dish of recooked fish, often served for breakfast. Although fish was originally served with it, in India kedgeree refers to a mixture of rice cooked with butter and dhal, spices, and shredded onion.

MULLIGATAWNY
The well-known soup comes from the Tamil words *milaku tanni*, meaning pepper-water, and originated in Madras.

PAAN
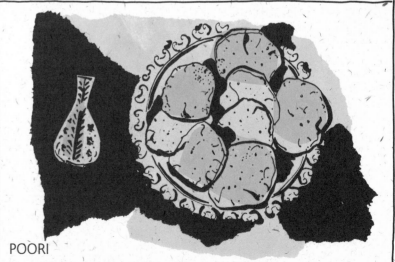
Betel leaves folded over to enclose spices and dried areca nuts, used as a digestive.

PAPADUM
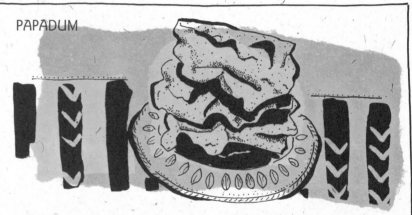
A flat, thin, deep-fried wafer usually made from split peas or potatoes. It can also be made from any kind of pulse or lentil flour, seasoned with asafetida. In Bombay it is called popper cake; in Madras, *poppadam*.

POORI
Deep-fried bread that puffs up like a small balloon.

SHERBET
In Indian usage a drink of sugar and water, or syrup, but also used for drinks made with a mixture of wine or liquor.

THAL
A round dish made of silver, copper, or brass, usually used to serve vegetarian meals, called *thali*.

FURNISHINGS

CHARPOY
A lightweight cot or bed, common throughout India. Sometimes made in simple materials, at other times it can be elaborately painted.

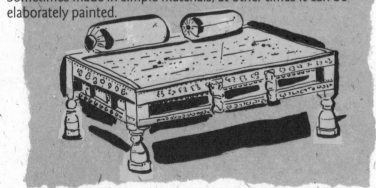

CHOKI
A rectangular-shaped unit that is used for cooking, storing, and washing.

COIR
Matting made from the outside fiber of the coconut.

DHURRIE
A flat woven cotton carpet, one of the oldest and most common types made in India by all religious groups and castes.

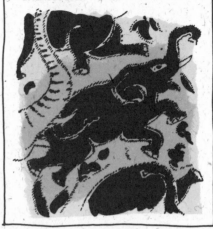

DOLLY
Adapted by the English from the Hindi word *dali*, it refers to a gift or presentation of fruit, flowers, vegetables, or sweets, sometimes arranged in a basket or on a tray. The gardener would offer his daily array of garden produce to the owner in this way.

JALI
A pierced screen.

JHAROKHA
An elaborately carved, partly enclosed balcony.

KOTHAR
A grain chest, colorfully decorated in style typical of the Kutch area.

HOOKAH
Hubble-bubble or pipe for smoking water-filtered marijuana or a mixture of tobacco, spices, molasses, and fruit.

PUNKAH

A large, portable fan or cloth-covered rectangular frame hung from the ceiling, pulled by a rope, to fan a room. The first versions were portable, made from the palmyra leaf.

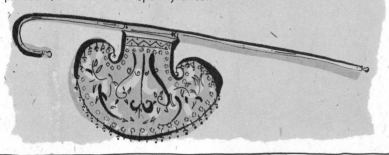

CATAMARAN

A raft or float made from wood tied together that is derived from the Tamil word *kattumaram*.

DINGHY

From the Bengal word *dingi*, an East Indian rowing boat. Sometimes also a canoe carved from the trunk of a tree. Now used for a small naval or civilian boat.

B O A T S

SOCHOK

A small table with detailed decorations that folds for travel.

DUNGA

Small, permanently moored houseboat, traditionally lived on by the poor in Kashmir.

TEA CADDY

A tin or box to contain tea. It derives from the Malay word *kati*, or *catty*, a weight of one and one third pounds. A catty box was often used for tea.

SHIKARA

A long, shallow boat used for transporting passengers, or laden with fruit and flowers for sale to the houseboats on the lakes in Srinagar.

ARCHITECTURE

BALCAO

A dominant element in Goan architecture. A columned porch, usually with a pyramidal roof jutting out from the front of the house, it provides seats on either side and is an ideal meeting or observation point.

BUNGA

A desert hut, with a main living space that is three to five meters in diameter.

BUNGALOW

From the Bengali word for hut, *bangala*. An Anglo-Indian one-story house surrounded by a veranda.

DURBAR

Originally the court of an Indian prince, now a ceremonial audience chamber.

POL

A tenement or densely packed housing, typical of India's large urban areas.

PURDAH

A Hindi word, from the Persian *parda*, an area in the house reserved for women and screened from the sight of men by a curtain.

VERANDA

An open, covered gallery that encircles bungalows and other Indian houses.

TEXTILES

BATIK

A textile dying technique in which areas not to be dyed are coated with wax, producing an irregular, mottled pattern.

BANDANA

A bright yellow or red silk handkerchief with diamond spots left white by pressure applied to prevent their receiving the dye. The word comes from the Hindi *badhnu*, which means to tie-dye. The caste in Gujarat who does this dying is called *banhara*.

CALICO

A white or small-patterned cotton cloth first imported from Calicut, India. Fine cotton material was originally mentioned by Marco Polo in the 14th century.

CHINT OR CHINTZ

The overall-patterned, often flower-covered, block-printed cotton fabric that has become synonymous with English-style decorating. Originally from the Sanskrit *chitra*, meaning variegated or speckled.

DHOTI

Fabric used for the long loincloth traditionally worn by Hindu men. It is wrapped around the body, with the end passed between the legs and tucked into the waist.

IKAT

Tie-dyed woven cotton or silk textile with colorful, intricate chevron patterns.

DUNGAREE

A coarse cotton fabric from East India that was traditionally worn by the poor. It is woven with two or more threads together in the warp and weft. The coarse varieties were used for sails for native boats and tents.

KANTHA

Rugs or embroidered quilts crafted from old saris, native to West Bengal.

MADRAS

A colorful plaid-patterned textile made of silk or cotton, or both, and colored with vegetable dyes. It takes its name from the southern city of Madras.

MUSLIN

Now refers to the thin, semi-transparent cotton cloth that was once made in Mosul in Iraq for the European markets and referred to as *musolins* by Marco Polo in 1298.

PAISLEY

An irregular tear-shaped pattern derived from the stylized mango that decorated the Kashmir shawls of India, which were later imitated in the Scottish town of Paisley.

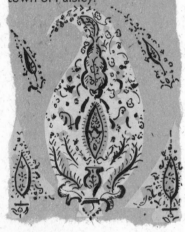

SAFA

A turban worn by a prince.

SARI

A traditional six-yard piece of pleated, folded, and tucked fabric worn by Hindu women since before 3000 B.C.

ZARDOZHI

The gold and silver sequin-covered embroidery made in Uttar Pradesh.

SARONG

An old Indian form of dress, later used only in the south. A body cloth or long kilt, tucked in at the waist, and generally of colored silk or cotton, it is the chief form of dress in Java and Malaya.

SITAR

A 700-year-old long-necked, stringed instrument, the most popular in India.

MUSIC

RAGA

A precise and complex melodic system of ascending and descending movement based on variations of 72 *melas*, or parent scales.

TABLA

Indian word for two drums, one played by the right hand and the other by the left.

TANPURA

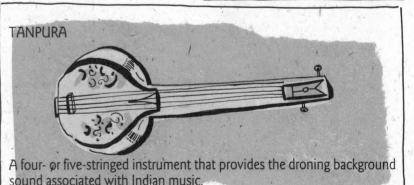

A four- or five-stringed instrument that provides the droning background sound associated with Indian music.

India is a land of festivals and fairs. Every day of the year there is a festival celebrated in some part of the country. Some festivals welcome the seasons of the year, the harvest, the rains, or the full moon. Others celebrate religious occasions, the birthdays of divine beings, saints, and gurus (revered teachers), or the advent of the new year. Some of the festivals are common to most parts of India.

Makara Sankranti marks the commencement of the sun's journey to the Northern Hemisphere and is a day of celebration all over the country. Wherever there are rivers or the sea, people take a dip in the waters on this day and worship the sun. In Gujarat, Makara Sankranti is celebrated by the flying of kites.

Republic Day is India's great national festival. The celebrations are most colorful in Delhi, the capital. On January 26 there are parades of the three armed forces, followed by floats and dancers from all parts of the country.

Vasant Panchami is a festival in honor of Saraswati, the goddess of wisdom and learning.

Maha Shivaratri is the night of the worship of the great Shiva, the third deity of the Hindu trinity. The pious stay awake all night and chant prayers. Usually there are fairs near temples for the entertainment of villagers during the daytime.

Holi is the spring festival and is celebrated with enthusiasm wherever there are cold winters and the end of the frost heralds the advent of spring.

Jamshed-i-Navroz is the New Year's Day for one group of Parsis; it goes back to the time of ancient Persia.

Mahavir Jayanti commemorates the birth anniversary of Mahavira, the founder of Jainism, a highly ascetic and austere religion that places great emphasis on Ahimsa, or nonviolence. It is a day of prayer. There are celebrations in all Jain temples and pilgrimages to Jain shrines.

Easter and **Good Friday** follow the same pattern of reverence and gaiety as in the West.

Baisakhi. All over the north the solar new year's day is observed on this day, which is also the new year's day of Tamil Nadu. For Hindus, it also denotes the days of the descent of the Ganges to the earth, and people take dips in rivers. For Sikhs, it is of special religious importance as the day of the formation of the Sikh Khalsa by Guru Gobind Singh, who converted the Sikhs into a martial race. It is also the harvest festival of the Punjab and is celebrated with dances and gaiety.

Ram Navami is the day of Rama's birth and is celebrated as a day of great piety, with the chanting of prayers and the singing of ballads.

Id-ul-Fitr or **Ramazan Id** marks the end of the month of Ramazan (Ramadan), the time when Muslims are expected to observe a strict fast from sunrise to sundown, in order to commemorate the descent of the Koran from heaven.

Raksha Bandhan is an integral part of the Hindu family structure whereby a woman ties a *rakhi* or decorative thread on the wrist of her brother to remind him to protect her if the need arises. The festival is celebrated as Coconut Day in Maharashtra as the monsoon seas are calmed by coconuts thrown to Varuna, the god of waters.

Independence Day, August 15, commemorates the day in 1947 when India achieved freedom. It is celebrated all over the country with meetings and flag-hoisting ceremonies.

Janmashtami celebrates the birth of Krishna, the eighth incarnation on earth of Lord Vishnu. It is celebrated by fasting, followed by feasting and merriment. Processions and floats are taken out and Ras-Lila, the folk dances of Krishna, are danced with great fervor, especially at places associated with the life of Krishna.

Id-ul-Zuha or **Bakrid** celebrates the sacrifice of Hazrat Ibrahim, who willingly agreed to kill his son at the behest of God. To celebrate the event, Muslims sacrifice one animal per family or group of families. There are prayers in mosques, feasting, and rejoicing. New clothes are worn and visits and greetings are exchanged.

Ganesh Chaturthi is celebrated in honor of Ganesha, the elephant-headed god who is worshiped as the remover of obstacles. In Maharashtra, huge images of Ganesha are carried in procession. On specific dates in the following ten days, these images are immersed in the sea or rivers with thousands of worshipers dancing and singing after them.

Navaratri/Dussehra/Durga Pooja. Navaratri, the Festival of Nine Nights, is celebrated in honor of the goddesses Durga, Laksmi, and Saraswati. The tenth day, Dussehra, commemorates the victory of Rama, of the epic Ramayana, over Ravana.

Diwali or **Deepavali,** the festival of "rows of lights," is the most important of all Hindu festivals. It is believed that it was on this day that Rama reentered Ayodhya after 14 years of exile. Deepavali is also celebrated as Naraka Chaturdashi, the day when the demon of darkness and dirt, Narakasura, was destroyed by Krishna. The celebrations commence with a purifying oil bath and the lighting of lamps, symbolic of the spiritual light pervading the earth and the destruction of darkness and ignorance.

Gurpurab. The birth anniversaries of Guru Nanak, the founder of Sikhism (October-November), and of Guru Gobind Singh, the last Guru (December-January), are important festivals of the Sikhs. In addition to the reading of the holy verses, the Guru Granth Sahib, the Sikh holy book, is carried in procession.

Christmas is widely celebrated all over India and is specially interesting in Goa and Kerala, where some of the local culture has been absorbed into the festivities.

SPECIAL LOCAL FESTIVALS

In addition to the festivals celebrated all over the country, there are local ones that are celebrations of special events like the New Year, harvest, birthdays of saints, etc. Some are temple festivals, religious events accompanied by music, dance, and gaiety. In many temples, images are taken in procession in chariots pulled through the streets by devotees. Most temple festivals are accompanied by village fairs, cattle, camel, or elephant fairs, and last three days to a month.

INDEX

STYLE LIBRARY

An ongoing series of high-quality all-color publications that focus on international areas of cultural and domestic interest.

French Style

Suzanne Slesin and Stafford Cliff/Photographs by Jacques Dirand

"Not only an important contribution to the literature of interior decorating, but also a touchstone for our times." – Los Angeles Herald Examiner

For centuries the French have been celebrated for their *art de vivre*, and *French Style* is a book that captures the charm, vitality, and elegance of the contemporary French life-style as it is reflected in that country's interiors. Town and country houses, flats, lofts, ateliers, and chateaus demonstrate the range of French design tastes and provide many translatable decorating ideas. *French Style* exudes that special quality, a rare blend of magic, elegance, and sophistication for which the French are famous.

The directory provides a listing of sources for French and French-style antiques and contemporary furnishings.

English Style

Suzanne Slesin and Stafford Cliff/Photographs by Ken Kirkwood

"A singularly beautiful and evocative look at the mix of formality, coziness, and comfort that is complex yet instantly recognizable as English Style." – Chicago Tribune

English Style richly illustrates the value of tradition and ingenuity in today's English interior design. From a grand manor house replete with chintzes to a London factory loft furnished with graphic severity, from a gabled country cottage to a Victorian terrace house with original William Morris wallpaper, each of these splendid interiors is quintessentially English.

More than 600 glorious full-color photographs accompany an informative text, and a catalogue of sources of English furnishings is included as well.

Like English literature and English manners, the English style of decorating has provided inspiration to generations of Americans and Europeans.

CARIBBEAN STYLE

Suzanne Slesin, Stafford Cliff, Jack Berthelot, Martine Gaumé, and Daniel Rozensztroch/Photographs by Gilles de Chabaneix

"A handsome book ... that presents the Caribbean islands as a rich and distinctive aesthetic experience." – New York Times Book Review

A unique blend of travel book and design book, *Caribbean Style* offers a previously unseen view of the architecture, interior design, gardens, and life-style of Guadeloupe, Martinique, St. Barthélemy, Antigua, Nevis, Montserrat, Barbados, Haiti, and Jamaica. The book includes chapters on plantation houses, town houses, popular houses, contemporary houses, gardens, island vegetation and colors, climate and crops, and cultural heritage.

With this vivid portait of the Caribbean, you will almost feel the soft breezes, inhale the fragrance of tropical flowers, and luxuriate in the warmth of the sun.

JAPANESE STYLE

Suzanne Slesin, Stafford Cliff, and Daniel Rozensztroch/Photographs by Gilles de Chabaneix

"A mesmerizing look at the rarefied and rarely visited Japanese homes." – Vogue

A stylish, sophisticated, and often unexpected look at how the Japanese live today, as expressed through interior design, *Japanese Style* captures the richness and diversity of modern Japan. In almost 800 full-color photographs, the book presents a wide range of houses and apartments – from architect-designed contemporary homes to centuries-old farmhouses and inns. The locations include a fashion designer's luxurious Tokyo duplex, a stunning house and garden on a hillside near Kyoto, a traditional geisha house, and the country house of the renowned potter Shoji Hamada.

Japanese Style holds many lessons – and delights – for Westerners as it evokes the never-ending romance of Japan.

Greek Style

Suzanne Slesin, Stafford Cliff, and Daniel Rozensztroch/Photographs by Gilles de Chabaneix

"Greek Style ... is almost as good as a vacation to that Mediterranean land." – Houston Chronicle

"The photographs ... are seductive ... what the simple rural style should be." – New York Times

Rustic and elegant, ancient and modern, minimal and yet rich in detail, the style of Greece is one of exciting contrasts. *Greek Style* captures not only the authentic simplicity of Greek interior design, but also the remarkable liveliness of Greek culture. Here you will discover the dramatic geographical range of Greece, from the northern mainland, with its mountains and Oriental influences, to the Cyclades, Ionian, and Dodecanese islands, with their whitewashed villages clinging to rocky hills. Centuries-old family estates, the turquoise and pink studio of a local artist, and the cliff-top and beach-front dwellings of newcomers – all celebrate an unforgettable and enduring stylistic tradition.